Marc Glorius (ed.)
Trans = Missions

AF284700

Marc Glorius (editor)

Trans =
Missions

- hand in hand -

Duino + Mostar
early years

various texts / various authors

Bibliografische Information der Deutschen Nationalbibliothek:
Die Deutsche Nationalbibliothek verzeichnet diese Publikation
in der deutschen Nationalbibliografie; detaillierte bibliografische
Daten sind im Internet über http://dnb.dnb.de abrufbar

© 2022: Marc Glorius
Layout und Satz: Martin Haeusler, Kerpen

Herstellung und Verlag: BoD - Books on Demand
Norderstedt

ISBN: 9783756212873

Table of Contents

Manuel Fernandez Canque – Tanya Behrisch – Sara Payne – Marc Glorius – Marcel Mikolášik – Marcin Zaleski – Daria Miglietta Ferrari – Maria Gallotti – Marilli Genova – Darina Dujmic – Marina Macchiaiol – Marvic Francalanza – Jasmins Tanovic–Bratic – Massimo Lengo – Pastor Linda Theophilus – Kató Eszter – Patrik Brundin – Paul Birighitti – Laura Amescua – Mauro Casiraghi – Adriaan van Otterloo – Ceci Egan – Pedro Herrera-Iglesias – Demet Devrim Derbil – Jen Van Ellemeet – Renata Bolognini – Leonardo Casalino – Sergio Vasques – Gerhard Schneider – Mette Høie – Dhakshi Ravishankar – Diana Bebek Ivankovic – Nicholas Isaacs – Milorad Samardzic – Silva Tomanic Kis – Dr. Pilvi Torsti – Ximena Pineda – Giorgio Casanova – Giorgio Topa – Niovi Zarampouka-Chatzimanou – Wisam Shamroukh – Giulio Federico – Alain Mauri – Elaine Teo – Alex Neuber – Alexander Grubic Wirtz – Elma Mahmutovic – Yew Chin Tan Eugene – Michał Gwardyś – Amanda Fong – Amela Bozic – Amit Mohindra – Anders Dahlbeck – Ingrid Prytz Ohm – Anne Nielsen – Robert Tomalin – Roberta Secchi – Mohammed M. Obaid Shwani – John Alexandropoulos – Bora Toska – Branka Uskokovic Zizic – Frederico Rosei – Assia Brandrup – Attila Kovacs – Lu Xina Torres – Eugenio Filippi – Luiz Antonio Magalhaes – Julie Koch – Tvrtko Cernos

I. "Passing the baton"
Introduction

When David Sutcliffe died on the 11th of November 2019, Manuel Fernandez created, with others, the "Remembering David Sutcliffe" website on Facebook. The many tributes that were published on it "touched" me.

I recognised myself in them.
I also find them interesting as "genre".

The many alumni, colleagues, friends expressed deep feelings and thoughts – of gratitude, acknowledgement, and love.
Many of these would have been difficult to express during lifetimes.
One can see well out of these tributes what a profound experience the college years were and how lasting was the work of the educator David Sutcliffe.

When Manuel Fernandez approached me with a request to transpose these tributes out of the internet into a book I agreed to do so.
Assembled, these tributes together paint a big and strong picture like the small and colourful pieces of a mosaic.

I asked myself:
What kind of book would make sense?
What is this book for?

I started and realised, a simple collection of tributes would run the danger of fueling a cult of the personality (of David Sutcliffe).
This would not be in his sense, not in mine, not in the sense of the collegio.
What then is the purpose of this book?
What is the purpose of cultivating memory?

The following five aspects seem important to me:

1) Starting with the obvious: It is important to keep in memory that which is worth remembering.
And the colleges are worth remembering. Their memory is worth being carried on, their basic idea is worth being re-translated.
They are worthy of continuing to exist.

2) The idea of the school, its essence, is valuable.
"Essence" is immaterial. One cannot easily touch it.
One needs to reflect on it, turn around it, define it again and again and translate into the different contexts.
We have terms like: "international understanding", "bridging cultures", "living and learning together", "experiential education", "intesa-dia-logue".
The words highlight one part of the idea of the school.
The selection of texts in this book highlights other sides of it too.
The texts try to turn around the essence.
The colleges need to relate to the idea of the school and stand in a constant feedback loop to it.

3) If you talk about the colleges, especially the one in Duino, then one talks about David Sutcliffe as its founder and first headmaster.
Many more have contributed to its creation.

In general, I don't think that anything can be created by one person alone: "No one succeeds alone." (Robert L. Reffkin)
Everything gets created in cooperation, in context, in a "field".
There are contributions of Elisabeth Sutclffe and teachers of the first generation: Franziska Raimund, Manuel Fernandez, John Plommer, Walther Hetzer.
There are contributions of the poet and ex-bartender of Bar Europa Lucia – Lussia di Uanis and of the poet and husband of Franziska: Hans Raimund.

Other contributions of the "field" are texts of co-years of mine talking about their lives in connection with the college experience.
There are poems, essays, some photos and quotes.
The Bora, the strong coastal wind gets mentioned repeatedly, the Adriatic sea, the carso, Duino, its inhabitants and its special atmosphere.
It was important for me to let the field get expressed.

4) How does it continue in Duino? How does the college develop?
How does an adequate perspective of the future look like?
Where does it go to?

5) Question number five: What does remain?
In analogy to the seasons of the year I am talking of autumn and winter.
What remains after death?
David Sutcliffe – the founder – left.
Elham Sheiry of the first teacher generation died not long ago.
Maria Teresa Visintin died in 1987.
Of the generations of my times Bernd Weiler, Dino Stanic, Giorgio Baschiarotti and Matteo Troni left.
All of us will follow.
What remains of the persons and their work after they have left?

I like watching the leaves falling in autumn.
They cover the soil, protect and nourish it.
The trees extract what they need from the soil and continue growing.
This book is a container of memory and perspective.
Metaphorically speaking it can contribute to feed the soil of the college.
This is less about nostalgia; it is more about the rear-view mirror.
Let's take the image of driving a car and looking into the rear-view mirror while looking ahead.
The basis is a car driving in a wanted direction, in other words:
Movement following intention.

"I regard it as the foremost task of education to insure the survival of these qualities: an enterprising curiosity, an undefeatable spirit, tenacity in pursuit, readiness for sensible self denial, and above all, compassion."

(Kurt Hahn)

Contributes
Poems
Essays

Lucia Pinat
Franziska Raimund
Marc Glorius
Walther Hetzer
John Plommer
Cesare Onestini
Roberta Secchi
Hans Raimund
Peter Senge
Elisabeth Sutcliffe
Ayman Allo
Felix Klein
Manuel Fernandez
Yves Aka
Cornelia Vospernik

"Your disability is your opportunity" (Kurt Hahn)

Preface

In this chapter different kinds of texts are gathered. Some – the con-tributes – were directly written on the occasion of this book. Others – the poems and essays – were written in the course of the years on different occasions.

In the contributes ex-students and teachers of the first generations are telling about their college experience and their lives.

The teachers contributing are Walther Hetzer, John Plommer and Franziska Raimund.

The ex-students contributing are Yves Aka, Aiman Allo, Felix Klein, Cesare Onestini, Roberta Secchi and Cornelia Vospernik.

The sample of voices is „representative in its subjectivity". What I want to say with this is that alumni and teachers were there in the eight-ies, the time I went to college. I know them all personally.

The contributions of Lucia Pinat and Elisabeth Sutcliffe are a little different. The artist and poetess Lucia Pinat worked as a bartender at Bar Europa in front of the administration building and Elisabeth Sutcliffe is the widow of David Sutcliffe and has dedicated her entire life to the UWCs. She has been there since the beginnings of Atlantic College in Wales.

The poems are of Hans Raimund, husband of Franziska Raimund and a renowned and award winning Austrian poet, of Lucia Pinat and of Marc Glorius. They are in Italian, English and German.

The essays are mixed:

In "2913 km" Marc Glorius is telling a road trip to the UWC Mostar in Bosnia-Herzegovina.

There is a historical essay on Duino by Walther Hetzer talking about the wounds the several wars left in the region.

The essay "10 day ago I had a phone call" of Manuel Fernandez is written in the moment when he hears that the social services of the college in Duino are in danger.

The essay of Peter Senge differs from the rest as Peter Senge is not connected to the UWCs. Specialised on learning organizations he is senior lecturer at MIT and a renowned author. The text is a transcript of a speech of Peter Senge in which he exposes how one can recognize a vision shared by many people.

Lucia Pinat/Lussia di Uanis

"these cliffs well-known to us,
in a hypothetical, lost blue

and yet when I see them
I tremble in my intimate

like dissolving memories
in the distance"

When I think of Duino these verses come into my mind. I wrote them during those years on a sketch that represented the castle on the cliffs – in overseas blue.

On these inaccessible cliffs that lean on the Duinese sea, it is not Rilke who put the angels but they have always been there. I think that in their brightest smiles vibrates the wave of our young days and in their stormy looks, when the Bora howls through the sharp rocks and the rocks sing together of all the lives they have known.

I arrived to Duino from the Bassa Friulana. Even if that territory was so nearby to mine, it is very different, with the rugged and intense colors of the Carso that is embracing it with these stones in rough and cutting forms. They have always made me shiver.

And then in Duino there is the sea, since ever desired and dreamt of. I was restless, full of dreams. I wanted to paint, become an artist. I wanted to have my say, express myself.

I needed to find a work though, a house, go away from my parents. I had a car, I could move. I found work as bartender at Bar Europa (the actual Mickey Mouse) in the evening hours from 5 to 12 pm and longer. Bar Europa was a normal coffee and panino place like any other. But as it was located in front of the office building of the Collegio del Mondo

Unito it was a portal opening to the world, a meeting point of the villagers, a majority of them spoke Slovene as mother tongue, of all the languages of the world. The language of the "ragazzi" and the teachers of course was English and I couldn't speak it, anyway, all of them also learned Italian soon. The bar turned into a retreat sometimes, to be out of the system, to take a break, to meet, a place from where to look at truths from a different angle or to get to know local people.

I had an extraordinary collection of musical tapes with me – in a big plastic bag – with the music I listened to in these years: The Talking Heads, Clash, Dire Straits, Police, Style Council, Soft Cell …

I put this music as the soundtrack of the evenings in the bar. I suspect it contributed quite a bit to give birth to extraordinary still lasting friendships. I remember once my affacionados of the College invited me to be part of a team for a relay race in the village that gathered students and villagers. Our group's name was with some irony: "With Lucia. Without Energy"

Friendships of these times have remained in the hearts even though each of us has been following his own road. Still the roads still meet once in a while and then words and visions confront and meet and we exchange opinions on life. I know for sure that I have been "home" for some. I have been hostess and guest, marriage witness, work colleague and travel mate. I have been "ritorno".

I believe that we all live in the memories of these cliffs leaning vertically on the sea, in the vibrating light of that blue Novalis recalled in "azzurre lontananze" blue distances.

Lussia di Uanis/Lucia Pinat
Native Italian
85-88 Bartender at Bar Europa/Duino Visual and performing artist,
poetess, writer
Writing in Italian + Friulano
Currently living near Udine/Italy

David B. Sutcliffe (DBS) – A man with a vision

Franziska Raimund

I had my first encounter with DBS in Vienna, at the Ministry of Education. David was there in order to select a teacher for German and French together with two Austrian officials. The College was in its second year and Austria had decided to support it by sending and paying for an Austrian teacher.

To my great surprise, DBS chose me although two male colleagues were equally qualified. The reason for his decision must have been the fact that I wanted to come with my family – with Hans, my husband, a poet, translator and pianist, our young daughter Henny and our dog. Maybe also because like David I speak four languages (German, French, Italian, English).

In 1984 we arrived in Duino. The beauty of the place enchanted us. The busy life at the College was first a little shock and then a great challenge. DBS proved to be an efficient headmaster, respected, often admired, showing the right attitude in the right moment, dealing with teachers and students in a way we all could accept.

The first years in the College were an adventure for all of us. Everything had to be planned, created, implemented, realised … We lived in a permanently exciting and exited atmosphere. We all felt like pioneers. The many qualities of my students impressed me. They were enthusiastic, open-minded, gifted, willing to work – a pedagogic paradise. (When at the end of my first year one of my German students was awarded not only the top grade for his IB exam in German but also the distinction „outstanding", DBS called me in his office and thanked me. I felt accepted and was grateful.)

Very soon I created a very unconventional, unusual, big language department. My idea was to offer the possibility to continue their language and literature studies to the majority of students with a mother tongue other than English or Italian, German or Spanish (which were regularly taught languages). I wanted them not to forget their roots. I looked for highly qualified „language tutors" who came at weekends (from Trieste, Gorizia, Venice, Bologna, Milan, Budapest etc. – The Finnish teacher came from Vienna, the Japanese from Belgrade) to meet their students. I organised workshops for them and instructed them how to teach the IB programme. Many students were grateful to be in contact with at least one adult person with the same cultural background. Soon 25 teachers for 25 languages were employed.

I would like to name all languages of that fantastic department:

Albanian, Arabic, Bulgarian, Chinese, Croatian, Czek, Danish, Dutch, Finnish, French, Hebrew, Hungarian, Japanese, Macedonian, Modern Greek, Norwegian, Polish, Portuguese, Romanian, Russian, Serbian, Slovak, Slovene, Swedish, Turkish.

I thought that this admittedly very expensive department was important for an international College like ours. DBS shared my view. He called the language department „il fiore all'occhiello" – one of the main special characteristics of the College which distinguished it from all other Colleges. At the end of the Academic Year he invited all language tutors to a fabulous dinner at the Dama Bianca – unforgettable evenings!

As far as I know this wonderful language department has been completely destroyed after my return to Austria in 1997. For financial reasons, they say.

I'll always remember a student from Canada, Chrystia Freeland, who asked me (at that time I was Director of Studies) to introduce Ukrainian as a Language A, the language of her ancestors. The IB did not accept this. Until 2019 Chrystia was foreign minister in Canada, now she is Deputy Prime Minister and Minister for International Affairs.

My love of languages was also one of the reasons why I created „Poetry Workshop" as an aesthetic activity. Once a week, students assembled in our „tavernetta" and we read together selected poems by different authors in different languages and in translation. And then I invited the students to write their own texts in their own language and to provide a translation, if possible. We recited our texts and compared them. At the end of the year, we published a booklet „Sottovoce" with our poems. David was very much in favour of this activity and willingly offered the necessary money for the publication.

Hans' aesthetic activity was Chamber Music. He played the piano together with a violinist, a cellist and other instruments. Whenever he gave a concert with the students, David and Elisabeth were present and seemed to enjoy it.

Another very important and so to say unique enterprise was my creation of the so called „Duineser Gespräche" („Duinese Conversations"). I assembled teacher of German A in International Schools in Duino and held workshops concerning the IB programme, the selection of literature, the different ways to examine etc. This group became bigger every year. But the real asset was that I also invited the Chief Examiner of German A to attend our workshops. And he came. The IB office found this a scandal and was more than surprised. Nobody else had had this idea so far.

DBS found it a good idea and again proved to be very generous by inviting all of us to the Dama Bianca.

DBS had many excellent social and pedagogical qualities, but he was also an excellent business man. In my 13 years at the College I had so many tasks and duties like no other teacher: I was teacher of German A and B, French A and B, Head of the above mentioned Language Department, Director of Studies, IB Coordinator, Deputy Head, Activity leader and Tutor. As a seconded teacher I was paid by the Austrian Ministry of Education.

After my leaving the College in 1997 all these duties were distributed among five or six different teachers. In retrospective I must say that I loved all these jobs.

I must admit that I don't know David as a private person very well. He kept other people so to say at a save distance, except a few close friends like the president of the College, Corrado Belci, or the bursar Giorgio Pontoni. He was friendly but never obtrusive, discreet but also approchable.

I remember two occasions when David openly showed that he was interested in our lives.

In 1994 Hans was awarded the prestigious „Georg-Trakl-Preis" for his poetry. The ceremony took place in Salzburg. David and Elisabeth travelled to Salzburg, joined us in the „Trakl-House" and came with us to a dinner offered by the city of Salzburg.

The second occasion was one year later when Hans' editor decided to celebrate Hans' 50th birthday in a characteristic restaurant with a group of literary people in Stanjel, Slovenia where all dishes were made of bear-meat – awful! David and Elisabeth were our good humoured guests.

On one occasion he revealed his inner self to me. This was when he and Elisabeth decided to spend a whole year in England in order to be able to be with their youngest son Edward who was very ill and passed away in their presence. It was the year of the 10th Anniversary of the College, a year of many special events. David asked me if I could replace him, take over his duties and be the Acting Head. I agreed without thinking about it twice. I treasure his letter of gratitude.

As a headmaster David was very strict in two respects: absolutely no drugs and all students had to come there with a scholarship of their country or other sponsors. Not one student should be there because her or his parents were rich and could afford to pay for the very costly two years at the College.

As far as I know this policy came to an end. The College in Duino accepts now also paying students.

Another very important area for David was the good communication and friendly relationship with the people of Duino. Teachers and students were invited to take part in these attempts. The result was fabulous. Several times almost all inhabitants of Duino accompanied the College on their trip to the different places where the Opening of the Academic Year took place (Budapest, Vienna, Geneva, Rome etc.). They all loved David for his modesty, concern and friendliness. The students were invited by the families and contributed a lot to the wonderful atmosphere in the village.

Again, as far as I know, now there is no longer a warm relationship between the College and the Duinese people. This is in my view really a pity. But if the headmaster is not interested why should the students care?

Looking back gratefully at our time in Duino, at our years at the College, Hans and I agree that these 13 years have been the best years of our life. And David has been a very important part of it…

* *Franziska Raimund Native Austrian UWCAD 84-97 (Teacher)*
Franziska taught German and French, was Director of Studies, created a memorable Language Department and memorable poetry workshops in Duino
Translator
Currently living in the Burgenland near Vienna/Austria

Marc Glorius

Mi manca il mare (2004)

La chimica creata al collegio è stata unica.
Sono stato triste come la guerra
quando l'ho lasciato.
Con tutti gli amici.
Verdad

Mal di mare
ferita
un' esperienza
difficilissima ad integrare
nulla la vita che seguiva

Esperienza
come il vento della Bora....violenta.
Voci profonde svegliate,
entusiasmanti appassionate
art brut
la vita è sogno

Esperienza che non mi ha dato pero
insegnamenti
sulle esperienze sconvolgenti....
delle chiavi perché aprino
le *mie porte*

Per tanti anni
al fondo dei miei sentimenti
questa sensazione di
casa – ritrovata, e poi.... *persa*
di nuovo, again.

Soltanto molto dopo ho capito:
Il tessuto degli anni di Duino fu
una vera vela arcobalena
per cui ho dovuto creare io
una nave adatta.

Gli manca il mare

* Marc Glorius
Native French/German
UWCAD 86-88 (Student)
Writer, teacher and entrepreneur,
25 years of practice of martial arts
and meditation
Currently living on the border of
Germany, France and Switzerland

Walther Hetzer

Historical

Trenches (always difficult to dig in the hard limestone) and fortifications of both World Wars are everywhere around Duino, mixed with the natural *dolinas* so typical of the Karst. My students at the time diligently traced some of them, both for the history classes as well as for creating accurate maps for orienteering competitions. *Mount Ermada*, key point of some of the *Isonzo* battles, is close by, dominating the Karst.

The Austrians transformed it into a major bulwark against Italian assaults. There is a photograph of the building, now housing most of the classrooms of the UWC of the Adriatic. In Austrian hands in 1917, Duino was shelled heavily prior to the last Italian offensive. In the image, a huge shell hole shows in the roof of the building, right above where we held our class that was to explore the causes of war many years later.

Before the war, Rainer Maria Rilke, one of the greatest poets, was a visitor at Duino Castle in 1912, a guest of Princess Marie von Thurn und Taxis. There he started writing his *Duino Elegies*. The Great War affected Rilke deeply and the *Elegies* remained unfinished and unpublished until 1923. The *Sentiero Rilke*, a wonderful footpath along the coastal cliffs, offers views of the Carso and the Bay of Trieste in the distance, the white speck of *Miramare Castle* clearly visible at the entrance to the bay. It was built for Emperor Franz Joseph's brother, Archduke Maximilian, who was shot in *Querétaro* as Emperor of Mexico. *Miramare* hosted Franz Ferdinand for two months in the spring of 1914, before he went off to Sarajevo in July for his fateful encounter with the three nineteen year old youths, now alternately called terrorists or freedom fighters. Gavril Princip and his companions seem curiously similar in their mixture of gullibility, idealism, naivety and lack of prospects to some of the youths drawn to radical causes today.

Not far from Duino are two other sites and images with diametrically opposed effect on me: Redipuglia and San Martino del Carso. The guidebooks state with uncanny precision that Italy's largest war *sacrarium* in Redipuglia contains the corpses of 39,857 identified Italian soldiers and 69,330 unidentified. In a nearby cemetery, around 14,000 Austro-Hungarian soldiers are buried. Inaugurated in September 1938 with Mussolini in attendance, its 22 gigantic stone steps are pure fascist architecture. The immense 75 ton porphyry sarcophagus of the Duke of Aosta, commander of the 3rd Army, flanked by the tombs of four of his generals, holds undisputable pride of place. The roll call of *"Presente"* is carved with endless repetition in the rising steps. "Presente, presente, presente." In the commemorative park an inscription: *"Dulce et decorum est pro patria mori."* I resisted the temptation to tell my students how deeply repulsive this gigantic heap of stones is to me.

Historical echoes resonate easily in this border country. On top of the hill there is a column, brought there from the nearby military and commercial Roman center of *Aquilea*, meant to commemorate the victims of all wars. It is more touching than the gigantesque glorification below. At the nearby mouth of the *Timavo* river, already prominent in Virgil's poems, a bronze sculpture of the *Lupi di Toscana*, the Tuscan Wolves of military fame during Italy's wars of independence, looks out over an original section of the Roman Road, the *Via Timavo* of AD 200. It also points up to the slopes of *Mount Ermada*. A couple of hundred meters up from there is a small and unheralded grotto containing the remains of an altar of Mitra, the Persian cult popular with the Roman legions of the time.

Layers and layers of history, layers and layers of wars, borders and demarcations exist. With the collapse of the Austro-Hungarian monarchy, the borders around Duino were set in the Paris treaties, with Italy receiving parts of *Friuli/Venezia Giulia*. From then on, Trieste with its Piazza Unita D'Italia was considered sacred nationalist territory by the Italian right. Istria, still ancestral home of Italian fishermen settling there since Venetian times, and much of the Dalmatian coast below it went to Croatia. My history students traced the post World War One maps, already aware that equally complicated tasks lay ahead, namely sorting out the arrangements in the region after 1945.

Establishing borders after the Second World War was extremely difficult in some areas and took longer than the arrangements made after 1918. Only in 1975 was the *Treaty of Osimo* signed by Yugoslavia and Italy, dividing what had been the *"Free Territory of Trieste."* After 1954, Italy had provisionally administered Zone A and Yugoslavia had administered Zone B. In class, instead of following the trenches and battle lines of the First World War, we traced the ethnic complications created by these Zones, replete with new nationalistic and linguistic divisions still lingering today in Duino and the region.

The president of the UWC of the Adriatic, the former Italian parliamentarian Corrado Belci, provided a strong personal connection. As a local politician he had been politically involved in the establishment of the Treaty of Osimo. At the time, sentiments of Italian right-wing nationalists resenting the recognition of the border resulted in death threats against him. Even late in the 80th, when the Duino students organised a charity march to the Piazza Unita D'Italia in Trieste, it was made clear to us that our student speaker Flavia, a Slovene speaking girl from Istria, should think carefully about uttering even one word in Slovene on that square. This could cause serious repercussions for her and the college. The school was ready to support her and left the decision to her. On the day, flanked by more than 100 flags representing our students, Flavia only spoke Italian.

Moving on to one more small digression in time, I think of lunch in the summer of 1991 with Slovene colleagues from Ljubljana and Maribor in the Istrian town of Piran. Fishermen were on this coast long before the Romans, Venice added beautiful buildings when it ruled the Adriatic, and Austria had its time here. We met at the end of a school year, as the end of Yugoslavia seemed near and Slovenia was about to declare its independence. None of us around the table knew what was going to happen. We did expect some crisis of words and a lot of political maneuvering, but could not imagine that yet another "Balkan War" was going to break out so soon. During the December break that followed, I went back to Duino and with a friend drove up from there to a small fogbound Croatian town in a van full of school supplies. The Serbs had just bombed the city of Vucovar; three-thousand refugees had found refuge in the local school. One of the children insisted I take a gift, a piece of wood into which he had driven nails to form a stag's head. Driving back across the Italian border, established with such difficulty years before and geographically so close, we exchanged the world of refugees for the affluent world of vacationers packing up their skis for the winter holiday.

History is personal history, full of images, memories, and emotions. We do not always know why some impressions resonate deeply with us. Maybe more than all those that I have mentioned above, I think of a plaque in the small village of San Martino del Carso. My students and I had walked there from a nearby mountain plateau, after visiting one of the sites of the first massive poison gas attacks on the Italian front. San Martino del Carso is a placid and attractive place, set in the grey limestone hills covered by red leafed scrub in the fall. It became the title of a poem by Giuseppe Ungaretti, displayed on an old wall at the entrance of the village. Both poem and plaque are more personal and vivid in my memory than most images of the Great War.

San Martino del Carso

Di queste case
non è rimasto
che qualche
brandello di muro

Di tanti
che mi corrispondevano
non m'è rimasto
neppure tanto

Ma nel mio cuore
nessuna croce manca

E' il mio cuore
il paese più straziato

...

Of these houses
nothing
but fragments of memory

Of all who
would talk with me not
one remains

But in my heart
no one's cross is missing
My heart is
the most tormented country of all

Giuseppe Ungaretti - Valloncello dell'Albergo Isolato, 27th August 1916. Translated from the Italian by David McDuff and Jon Silkin - from "The Penguin Book of First World War Poetry" edited by Jon Silkin

* Walther Hetzer Native Austrian
UWCAD 85-91 (Teacher)
Walther taught history and economics and was Director of Studies
in Duino. Leading educator on the field of international education,
passionate of photography, ecology and social justice
Currently living in Vienna/Austria

John Plommer

My Early Years at the United World College of the Adriatic

I arrived at the college in late August of 1986, after bureaucratic delays and long flights from Vancouver. It was hot as hades, and I was whisked to the now-defunct Hotel Agip – then of course an important part of College life for food, national evenings and various other events. After a few days I was given my very pleasant apartment at the northwest entrance to Duino, and immediately I had two visitors who introduced themselves as two of my new tutees. Felix and Julia, second year students, had chosen me as a tutor because I was a Canadian, as they had an affinity for Canoes. They proceeded to fill me in on what to expect in the College, valuable information, indeed. As Richard van de Lagemaat said to me at the time "When you first arrive as a teacher, you know nothing, and the second-year students know everything."

I had been expecting a tight-run ship, having visited Atlantic College nine years earlier as the guest of David Sutcliffe. There I had been very impressed by the capabilities of the students, and particularly with cliff and sea rescue, along with their incredible self-discipline. However, according to my Canadian former students at AC, there was very limited informal after-hours socializing in those days, and sexual encounters difficult to arrange. Nonetheless, they loved the College experience there. Adriatic College, however, was what the Duinesi called "il casino di Duino". Students seemed to have almost no supervision in the residences, though the residence tutors were caring and available. Students had no need to pay attention to supposed curfew and there were no limits on student drinking beyond an intolerance of drunkenness. However, drugs were a red line, and one of the few rules that was enforced.

Of course, I spoke to the Headmaster about the loose approach, and he said very frankly, that the Atlantic College model would not work in Duino, and that he was wary of having "too many rules". Over the years the College did tighten up somewhat, and I think today it is a more disciplined and ordered place. One very liberal friend of mine who came to visit in the early days, someone who was an experienced social worker with teenagers and who had operated several group homes, took one look and said, "I do not think it such a good idea to let a bunch of sixteen- and seventeen-year-olds do exactly what they please." Perhaps not, but the environment was surprisingly self-ordered, something approximating what anarchists like to imagine as how to run a society without rules.

Students did figure out in each residence how to have some form of common understanding about how to live together, and that was very positive. I always felt welcome visiting the residences, but I never went there after ten in the evening, not at that time being a residence tutor. Of course, having a large corps of cleaning ladies helped. The scenes in the kitchens and bathrooms could be rather horrendous. In some residences I do not think a single plate or cup was every washed by students. In others, and particularly the smaller residences, I think there was more consensus and better upkeep.

Immediately upon arrival I was drafted for the Marine Activities Programme, working with Mark Bannar-Martin, Richard van de Lagemaat, David Sutcliffe and Edward Sutcliffe along with several other students. With canoeing (or kayaking as a Canadian would call it) I had no problems, being well-experienced. I also had swimming and lifesaving certification from the Red Cross. I had sailed, but I had no certification or teaching experience, and being thrust out as a sailing instructor in seas with unpredictable winds, I consider in retrospect to have been ill-advised and perhaps bordering on the irresponsible.

2/

However, no one drowned, and I know I was overly cautious about going out in chancy weather. I remember that on one occasion working with Edward Sutcliffe, I decided that day not to let the students sail. He, a thousand times more experienced than I, accepted my decision – albeit I could tell he thought it was wrong. He knew that as a staff member, I was the one responsible for any misfortune, and I admired him for his forbearance with my caution and for his empathy and understanding. He was a fine person.

The official opening of the College academic year was held later that autumn and we travelled to Rome via Florence, and I tasted the full College experience. In Florence there was a great ceremony in the grand hall of the Palazzo Vecchio. The Mayor and several others made laudatory speeches about the College. Trumpets blared, Florentine colourful banners were unfurled, and the students marched into the hall carrying their national flags in procession.

The Mayor and several others made laudatory speeches about the College. I was busy learning Italian, and I remembered the Mayor referring to "Questi splendidi ragazzi del Collegio del Mondo Unito". The phrase stuck in my mind, and I often used it to tease and shame the students, *gli splendidi*, into living up to their reputations. Of course, they were splendid young people, but I do not think it did them much good to be told that without emphasizing the responsibility that is placed on gifted people, but perhaps that is just my Canadian puritanism speaking.

I remember chatting with David Sutcliffe about the impression the flag procession made, and his comment gave me a real inkling into some of the conflicted viewpoints that one could hold in such an institution. He said he always felt quite uneasy about the flags, as flag-waving is so closely associated with nationalism, and of course nationalism when it gets out of hand is the enemy of peace. Food for thought. Naturally, he wanted the students to have pride in their backgrounds and identities, and most of all to fight the temptation to be co-opted by so-called Western values. This was epitomised by his encouragement of students to return to their home countries for university studies, but of course in many ways he fought a losing battle, especially as the IB and the UWC movement came to be highly regarded by British and US and Canadian universities, and the scholarships flowed in.

But on to Rome, where of course there was another ceremony and a visit to the Senate and to the Quirinale to meet the President. We were real VIPs. However, the whole expedition was very badly run, with coaches disappearing and arriving late, poor communication with the hostels where we stayed and much more. I did complain, and of course was immediately conscripted to the teams organizing several such trips in the future. That I did not mind, as in that area I did have a lot of successful experience, and I was glad to lend a hand. I think that these trips to inaugurate formally the academic year – to Vienna, Budapest, Milan and especially the mega-journey to Munich, Stuttgart, Geneva and Strasbourg – were among the most memorable experiences for everyone.

One anecdote from my Italian class with Fiorella: I sat at the back of the small room, and in front of me were a group of somewhat naughty and not-very-interested boys and at the front the rather sweet, studious girls. Having just arrived, I was very motivated to learn Italian, but it was also great to be mixed as a learner with the students in the class. Fiorella would tease the boys incessantly, and when they had acted up sufficiently, she would take a deep breath, expand her chest, stand on her tiptoes, and bark out in the loudest possible voice, aimed at the back of the room, "BASTA!". Of course, the boys would shrivel and get down to reciting the present tense of the first conjugation.

3/

I had left Canada in mid-life, giving up a very successful career there, including a headship, but I never regretted my move to Duino for a moment. I fell in love with Italy, warts and all, and I remain both chronically enchanted by *il bel paese* and yet often frustrated by some aspects to this day.

Of course, many Italians feel the same way, and all countries have their virtues and defects. I had left a series of tumultuous years on a personal level behind in Canada, and the College was a place where I could throw myself into my very rewarding work with a fabulous group of students and colleagues.

The intensity, the warmth, the love that existed cannot really be understood by anyone who had not been in the centre of that chaotic, yet overwhelmingly enriching and sustaining milieu.

* John Plommer
Native Canadian
UWCAD 86-96 (Teacher)
John taught history and economics in Duino and created the "World Art and Culture Course" for the IB
Currently living in Victoria/Canada and Milano/Italy

Marc Glorius

12,5 criteria defining a UWC and 2,5 criteria added (2017)

1) Boarding school

2) Scholarship based

3) Outstanding "location"

4) Highly international, heterogeneous backgrounds

5) IB – International Baccalaureate that opens the possibility to study worldwide, English as official language

6) Excellent "academics": Small classes, all kinds of learning opportunities, very good teachers

7) Based on the experiential pedagogy of Kurt Hahn (services, projects, activities)

8) Value-based: Committed to the experience and exploration of values like interculturality, difference, respect, responsibility and service.

9) Intention/mission: UWC contributes to a humanity that is capable of living in harmony with itself and the planet earth.

10) Experience of the world/pluriperspectivism: By living together the student experiences first hand a multitude of different cultural, national, social, individual perspectives.

11) Community-experience: Living together enables social experiences that can make the individual student grow considerably – highly valuable in our times of mini-families

12) Opens the possibility to study abroad

13) Individual support: The student with their talents, personality and difficulties is supported in order to allow him to live up to their potential

14) Outstanding teacher personalities who work under very good conditions and get coached themselves

15) Reflexiveness: Practicing a "spiritual" discipline chosen by the student to strengthen their capacity to reflect experiences and inner processes, to process information and maintain focus and attention. By teaching mindful practices the student gets "tools" that enable in a reliable orientation in his adult life

* *see further up*

Cesare Onestini

How many words has English?

Which language has more words, Italian or English? This was the first question DBS asked me – never mind it was part of an interview to get a life-changing scholarship and that I could hardly understand his native accent ... never mind that my confident reply was immediately shot down to reveal not only that English had more vocabulary but in fact so much more that there was no margin for error. This turned out to be a pattern when I got to UWCAD , the obvious question with the unexpected answer that pointed to a new way of thinking. Recasting expectations.

Years later I joined the „eurocracy" to work on intercultural educa-tion. It became for me the way to develop professionally in public ser-vice. Working in Brussels and serving on the UWC International Board brought together the continuity and the challenge of these two tracks.

Europe – or better the EU – built on principles of unity in diversity, promoting opening of education primarily across its member countries, moving important funds and anchored in the belief that building com-mon policies can prevent a return to war on our little continent. On the other hand UWC struggling with a global ideal in constant need of redefinition, depending on goodwill for its funding, changing the world one life at a time.

Many conversations with DBS in those years focused on this ques-tion: can we build bridges between the EU-ideals and its publicly fund-ed programmes and the UWC vision, its need for resources and its system of private schools.

We never really cracked that one either! But the question pushed the understanding of what was the real nature of the movement and the need for more innovation and risk taking in order to remain relevant and forward looking. It also helped me understand that the EU had its own trajectory, that as a political project it could not cater to all good ideas, but needed to focus on policies that could promote the common good, be amenable to political compromise and agreement, add value to the action of national and local governments.

English became ultimately a kind of a second mother tongue to me. Working in a multilingual environment for many years I also learnt that – yes, English might have the richest vocabulary – but we seem to use just a few – and always the same – words. It's what we make out of these words that can impact the future. One question at a time.

Cesare Onestini UWCAD 86-88 (student)
Native Italian
Cesare is working as Director General for Agriculture Fisheries, Social Affairs and Health at the General Secretariat of the Council of the EU
Currently living in Brussels

Roberta Secchi

Terribly afraid of indulging in rhetorical thoughts

Can we avoid fatefully laudatory pieces on such occasions, or are we bound to give mannered pictures of our past experience in Duino? One must accept the risk. Thirty-four years have gone by since I arrived in Duino. Duino is in Italy and I arrived there from my hometown which is also in Italy. Hey, but what a difference between these two Italies! From Sardinia to Friuli-Venezia Giulia, what a change! Still, the sea was there, a familiar friend suggesting the possibility of projecting one's aspirations towards the horizon and beyond it.

In the College I met adults who gave trust and encouragement at first glance. One would always have time to betray their expectations, of course, but that kind of start was giving impulse to 'lift the sails and catch the winds of destiny'. The message was: be confident! Try! A wider space opened for intuition and imagination to grow arms and hands and stretch them out. There were a lot of possibilities for the soul to touch, smell and taste the languages that have become the spinal cord of my life: visual arts, theatre, creative writing. Never before had I had so much time to dedicate to them within the school programme and not as extra-curricular activities.

Each of them was dignified by a competent adult through teaching, support, inspiration. There were students who had more talent, more dedication, better ideas than me and who pushed me to improve. I don't think I would have had the strength to pursue my artistic call without those two years of steady practice and growth. I was surrounded by commitment, I could equally see it in students, teachers and staff – not to mention DBS who was always there, as robust as the Castle rock. I was persuaded to do my best.

On the other hand, teachers were taking so much responsibility for their job that they could also utterly (and warmly) criticise my conduct: an Economics teacher wrote in the midterm report that 'Roberta cannot always hide her complete lack of interest in this subject'. When my father read this, he started to understand that I could not be forced into that direction. It makes me smile to think of this episode right now, but actually it has been quite a crucial turn on my road to empowerment.

Duino was "the place of others", people very different from me, walking mysteries speaking foreign verbal and non-verbal languages. At the beginning I was mostly in awe of them and feared the distance was too wide to be covered. Then curiosity came to my aid.

I wonder if I really didn't 'shrink and dread the chances'. Could I have done better then? Can I do better tomorrow? The legacy of those times is with me every time the Other meets me again.

(October 2020)

Roberta Secchi
UWCAD 86-88 (student)
Native Italian
Roberta is an art director, actress and teacher of theatre, art and creative writing
Currently living in Milano/Italy

Hans Raimund
(Duino/ Texte)

HIER WO

Die Alleen im Streulicht gilben
In abgesunkenen Gärten Rosen einzeln
Stehen verschossen rot gewärtig dass
Die Bora sie mit ihrer Schere schneidet
Die Kastanien sich im Regen schwärzen
Frost die Borke wetterseitig sprengt
Der Holzrauch übern mürben Rasen kriecht
Und sich verschlieft in triefenden Gebüschen
Im Finstern Katzen wie die Kinder greinen
Die Hunde vif das Laub durchstöbern
Die alten Fischer alte Netze flicken
Das Meer dem Horizont sein Wasser reicht
Nach Fellen Schwefel und Fäkalien riecht
Weit weg zu Gipfeln Eiszungen sich strecken
Über Klippen sich ein Regenbogen
Wölbt
          den ich erklimm und himmelquer
Bis an sein Ende geh und stets
Am Anfang steh

QUI DOVE

I viali nella luce diffusa indorano
Nei giardini sprofondati le rose sole
Rimangono rosso sbiadito in attesa che
La Bora con le sue forbici le tagli
Gli ippocastani nella pioggia si annerano
La corteccia volta a nord il gelo la spacca
Fumo di legna sui prati fradici striscia
E s'insinua nella boscaglia stillante
Gatti nel buio come bambini piangono
I cani vivacemente il fogliame frugano
Vecchi pescatori vecchie reti rattoppano
Il mare protende le sue acque all' orrizonte
Di pelle zolfo e feci odora
Lontano sulle vette lingue di ghiacciai si allungono
Sopra gli scogli un arcobaleno si
Inarca
       Che io scalo e attraverso il cielo
Fino al suo estremo mi spingo e ogni volta
All' inizio mi trovo

* Hans Raimund
UWCAD 84-97 (family member)
Native Austrian
Hans, the husband of Franziska Raimund, is a poet and translator
winner of numerous awards
Member of the European Academy of Science and Arts

Peter Senge

Shared visions

In fact, what often happens in organizations all the time, maybe you've lived through this, someone up here says hey, let me tell you about what our vision is. And just because they say it, it becomes the shared vision which of course isn't true at all. It's one person's vision, using their position of authority to act as if it's a shared vision. But in fact shared visions are real. And you've probably all heard that phrase.

And we found over the years, there's a couple of basics, that if people can start to get it, it really helps them a lot. The first is, there is always this interplay between the personal vision and the shared vision. To put it bluntly, if there are no personal visions, forget shared vision, really shared vision, not a facade, but the reality of shared vision. Because what brings people to work each day, what inspires them, is their own vision.

Personal visions are sort of like the soil nutrients, out of which you grow something called a shared vision. So you really are always in this territory of engaging people, talking about what they care about and then looking for ways that this can be aligned and assembled and put together, so there's something we're actually collectively caring about.

The one other thing we found very helpful that people, once they start to understand, is that diversity is actually part of shared vision. If you go and ask everybody, what's the vision, everybody uses the exact same words. I will tell you something, that is not a shared vision. People have memorised the correct words to talk about the vision. They're reciting the catechism, so to speak but by contrast, there is a whole that can start to emerge in a shared vision.

And the simplest way to understand that whole, we found over the years, is just to ponder, how does a hologram work. We've all seen the hologram, these three dimensional images which are quite remarkable, kind of walk around the side look at and you actually see it from a different angle when you walk right here. It really does appear to be three dimensional, in fact though, the physics of it is, it's being projected on a plate, on a two dimensional surface.

And the interesting thing about a hologram that really is instructive in understanding shared vision, is if you take that surface and you cut it in half, and you look at that half, you see the whole image, whatever that hologram is showing. You cut it in half again, so you've now got a quarter of that plate, you see the whole image. It's completely different than a photograph that way. If you cut a photograph in half, you see half the photograph. If you cut a quarter, you see a quarter of the photograph, but a hologram you don't, you see the whole of it.

But you actually see it from a slightly different point of view. It'll still seem three dimensional, but it's actually more limited. It's from a particular point of view. It's a little bit like if you pull a screen down over a window, you poke a hole in the screen, you see everything on the other side of that screen, but you see it from that point of view.

If you look at a hole over here, you see with another point of view. So shared visions are a little bit paradoxical in this sense, it really is about a hole, different people kind of holding a hole. That hole is the shared vision. But it's also about them seeing it from their unique point of view. It's not about repressing or covering up the fact that I see it this way, and you see it this way, and you see it this way.

So how to know there actually is a shared vision, is pretty simple. You watch if people are actually acting in a way that's bringing about something in the whole. There can be plenty of conflict, there can be obviously, lots of differences between what people see, how I articulate my vision of innovative school, how you do.

That's all different, because we have different points of view. But when it comes to action, there is a coherence to it. We're actually able to work together to bring it about. That's what you're really after in a shared vision, not everybody saying the same words.

* Peter Senge
Author of "The 5th discipline"
Senior lecturer at MIT, founding chair of the Society for Organizational Learning, Co-founder of the Academy for Systems Change

Elisabeth Sutcliffe

I want to thank Marc Glorius, Jale and Manuel Fernandez for producing this book. I greatly appreciate it and am pleased to see in it a more permanent memorial to David. I am also grateful for being asked to contribute to it.

I have been overwhelmed and deeply moved by the many tributes you made to David after his death: on Facebook, in cards, in letters and on the telephone. I am sorry I have not been able to answer them all, but I can assure you that they were and are a great comfort at a time when I feel a deep loss. I am extremely grateful for all your contributions. It was interesting to see what you thought David had taught you: aspire to freedom, but use it responsibly; be creative, but put ideas into practice, trust other people and they will respond to that; take up challenges to show that you can achieve more than you and others thought.

David would be pleased to know that the seed he planted in you is growing. I was touched to be mentioned in some of your tributes. I certainly tried to support David as much as I could, because I believed in him and his ideas, but I also sometimes had to bring him back to reality!

I know some of you lit candles in various churches for the two of us, and some attended a Memorial Service for David in the Duino Church, as others did for our son Edward in 1993.

A heartfelt thank-you to all of you.

Many of you knew David for two years, others for longer; I met him 61 years ago and was married to him for 58. We had a wonderful, varied and interesting life together in Wales, Italy and England. Apart from meeting you all we enjoyed our family life with Michael, Veronica and Edward, and later with Michael's and Veronica's spouses and children. David was tireless. Even in retirement he was one of the founders of the Mostar College, wrote several books on various subjects, and we travelled, went to museums, art galleries and theatres.

All our married life we had lived in Colleges, so we always had splendid surroundings, but never our own garden. Here in Sussex David taught himself gardening and re-designed our garden from scratch. One of his many challenges, which he met with great success!

He also had more time to play with his grandchildren than with our own children when they were young. In that way the whole family enjoyed his retirement, and so did he. He never stood still and continued to have new ideas and plans, until his illness took over, which was hard to accept for him and those around him.

Let us hope his ideas will live on, and this book will contribute to keeping his memory alive.

* Elisabeth Sutcliffe AC 62-82 UWCAD 83-01
Native German
Elisabeth was teacher, tutor and David Sutcliffe's wife
Currently living in Sussex/Great Britain

Walther Hetzer

What does Duino mean to me?

Coming from Vienna in 1985, I approached a place both real and saturated with myth. The area around Trieste, once the vanished Austro-Hungarian monarchy's access to the sea, drew Rilke, Joyce, Svevo, Magris and others – these great writers balanced the more sinister reminders of two world wars. When the school was founded, Gianni de Michelis, Italian Minister of Foreign Affairs, talked about rebuilding the pentagonale, the cultural union of countries forming Mitteleuropa. Ellen and I were drawn to this crossroad of Italian, Slav, and German culture.

We immediately loved the way the college was integrated within the whole village. We appreciated how close we were to students, as teachers and as house parents in the Foresteria and later in the Villa Lucchese.

When our first daughter Hannah was born in 1987, we had an endless supply of cheerful babysitters. Seeing our students not only in class, but also climbing with them on the nearby cliffs, skiing with them in many cross country races, sharing the weekly social service activities

… all this created attachments, which are still fondly remembered. Living in such a small place also led to a close-knit group of colleagues, working and private life not easy to separate.

As busy and intense life in a boarding school turns out to be, Duino also remains in memory as a beautiful place of leisure. Relaxing in the Bar Europa or at the porto, walking the Rilke path or up to the dolinas in the Carso, stopping for a chat anywhere in the village. Visitors to the college always remarked that our students approached them with ease, introduced themselves, and were happy to share something of their lives. For six years, Ellen and I were equally happy to share ours.

Duino is a place of enduring familiarity. Returning with my family a few years ago, with Hannah now an adult, we parked the car outside the admin-building. The door of the flower shop opposite opened, and the daughter of the owner emerged, about 30 years since we last saw each other. „Ciao Walther!" Elham Sheiry, the legendary Egyptian math teacher appeared from the plaza, ready to chat.

A magical place that evokes special memories.

* see further up

Lucia Pinat

Spesso la paura

Spesso la paura
ci fa lo sgambetto
e allora
cadiamo come pere mature sulla strada
Proviamo anora sgomento di essere su questa terra
e la terra sulla quale appoggiamo i piedi è solo terra
e non poema della vita.
Non riusciamo in quei momenti
a vedere più lontano del nostro naso
sentiamo soltanto male, male di vivere.
La nostra strada appoggiata sul filo lucente
diventa di ghiaccio, scivolosa
e i muscoli si irrigidiscono e
fa male anche muovere un dito.
Spesso
Sempre
dobbiamo rialzarci da soli
e la strada allora ritorna lucente
e la terra dove appoggiamo i piedi
poema della vita.

1995

* see further up

Marc Glorius

Cautious optimism – skeptical tradition

The educator Kurt Hahn developed his schools in order to create possibilities for a better future. His starting point was deeply felt suffering: from alienation from nature through industrialised societies, from the brutality humans are capable of within families, societies, dictatorships and wars.

Hahn invented the Atlantic College in Wales in reaction to World War II, Nazi and Communist dictatorships. Originally, the college was supposed to foster international understanding within western countries.

The purpose of all of his educational initiatives is to let the "good part" within humans thrive and persist. The background of this purpose is Hahn's awareness of how deeply rooted the forces of discrimination and destruction are within the human beings.

"*Penso positivo, ma non vuol dire che non ci vedo*" (Jovanotti 1994). "I think positive but this does not mean that I am blind" – a cautious optimism understands the ambiguity of human beings, is conscious of how deeply the barriers of class and race are anchored within, and is still capable of seeing the goodness in him; this seems to me a more realist view of humans than the "photoshopped" and overly enthusiastic idealism that is dominating UWC nowadays.

Such an idealism needs to remain on the surface as it does not give enough attention to the deep structures of humans.

It furthermore has the capacity to dissolve, the older one gets.

I don't want to be sarcastic or cynical here.

Not at all!

Enthusiasm for ideals, and experiences of love and harmony are great and precious. A "hurra-idealism" though comes too short, is easy to abuse and often crashes when confronted with the complex reality of the humans. Humans act rarely as they should act. "Apprehend the billy goat when it is in front of you, apprehend the horse when it is behind you, apprehend the human being from all the sides." (German saying)

Cautious optimism finds itself in acceptance of the human beings, the way they are. It is based on the observation and conviction that there is shadow and light in everyone.

Though light is more real than any form of suffering.

* *see further up*

Ayman Allo

November 1987

November 1987, I was late and I had to hurry up. It was my first time on a plane, and reaching Beirut airport was not as simply as it sounds. Yes, 5 o'clock in the morning, lots of military, and I was left by my mother on the airport entrance. She cannot go in ... it is forbidden. She gave me an important gift, 20 $, that was all she was able to provide. The only word that I had to remember was check in!. There with the only airline operating in Beirut ... Middle East Airlines, my adventure began.

I was late, I should have arrived 2 months before, but there was non possibility for a visa. "I should hurry, I am late!"

I arrived on the 11th of November, and it was nearly 11 p.m. I was given a bed. I knew that this was an important day for me. I felt it, it was so surreal, and I slept ... I was so tired.

The next morning I met you David. I thought "what an fascinating man, he looks cool, he has a hidden smile, and he looked at you in the eyes. A man of few words."

I needed a father guidance (I never really had one), and I felt it from the first day. He tried to hide it, and he tried to make me understand what has to be done and what has not to be done. What is appropriate and what is not. The messages were telegraphic or indirect, but the truth is that I never really listened. I believed and still believe in my instincts.

I made him smile once: There was a discussion in Foresteria about the Palestinian conflict, and at a certain point I expressed that a possible solution should be a 2 state solution. He said:

"What if they want it back later, they are much stronger than you"

I replied:

"It is like you are hungry, and you have to eat in Motel Agip, and there is one plate of overcooked pasta left. We have to share it, and I eat it so quickly, because I am so hungry, and even if the other guy wants it back, it would have been too late". He laughed, and I still remember his face.

I have so much to say about you Mr Sutcliffe, but I cannot express it in words, because you have left a mark which was implanted in me, and it was so difficult to adapt at the beginning, but I made it.

I am a self made man now for lots of reasons. You have had a part in this.

Take care ... I have to go, I am still in a hurry ...

* Ayman Allo
UWCAD 87-89 (student)
Native Palestinian
Ayman is a mathematician and entrepreneur
Currently living in Padova/Italy

Felix Klein

The experience of living and learning at the United World College of the Adriatic in Duino, for two years, was incisive for me – as it was for so many others. Although we had, of course, disputes and conflicts and heated political debates (the East-West conflict was still going on during my college years, socialist-ruled Yugoslavia was in the immediate vicinity), the atmosphere of tolerance and openness lived in Duino left a lasting impression on me.

Bringing students from all corners of the globe to live together in a UWC is certainly one of the best ways to immunize people against discrimination and racism for life. For me this experience also provided an important orientation for my choice of career. After graduating from Duino, I studied law in Freiburg in southern Germany, followed by a Master's degree in international law at the London School of Economics. Thereafter I successfully applied to the German Ministry of Foreign Affairs, where I held various positions in Germany and as a diplomat abroad.

In some of these positions I was involved in the international protection of human and civil rights, for example as a desk officer at the Foreign Office for relations between Germany and the Andean states of Bolivia, Peru and Ecuador, or as attaché for culture, press, and legal and consular affairs at the German Embassy in Yaoundé, Cameroon.

My experiences in these positions impressed on me again and again how important respect for human rights and the fight against all forms of discrimination are for the social cohesion of a country. When these conditions are in place, creativity and a political and social discourse, necessary for social transformation, peaceful coexistence and sustainable economic prosperity can best unfold.

In 2014, I was appointed Special Representative of the Federal Foreign Office for relations with Jewish organizations, the fight against anti-Semitism and for Holocaust remembrance at the international level.

These issues are of fundamental importance to the Federal Republic of Germany. This raison d'état for both domestic and foreign policy posits that the inconceivable crimes of National Socialism must never be repeated.

It is an ongoing political task for every German government and for German society to keep alive the memory of the atrocities of World War II and the Holocaust. Over decades the fight for its culture of remembrance has been fought in extremely controversial debates. Today, Germany is internationally highly respected for this culture of remembrance, and places a high value on international exchange.

Unfortunately, we have seen nowadays that despite all national and international measures, anti-Semitism has not disappeared and, in the age of the Internet and globalization, is resurgent in many countries, including Germany.

This was the reason that the German government decided in 2018 to create the new office of a Commissioner for Jewish Life and the Fight against anti-Semitism. I have now held this challenging office since May 2018. Anti-Semitism, hatred against Jews, is probably the oldest form of discrimination. It never ceases to amaze me how adaptable this hateful ideology is and how important it is for the state and society to take structural action against it.

I need to emphasize that anti-Semitism is not only directed against Jews, nor racism is only directed against people perceived as foreign, but against society as a whole, our way of life, our social diversity and ultimately our democracy. Someone who believes that sinister powers are "pulling the strings" in the background in parliaments, in the media or in economic life clearly has a problem with democracy.

In my office, I strive to coordinate government actions in the fight against anti-Semitism by bringing together government and civil society actors, educating the public through events and communication, and making proposals for new legislative and social initiatives.

It is important to show society that the fight against discrimination and exclusion concerns everyone and not just the affected groups. Even though my office is limited to the fight against hatred of Jews, I firmly believe that if we achieve success in the fight against anti-Semitism, we will also make progress in the fight against racism.

I am pleased to say that I have indeed succeeded in bringing about changes in the last three years in the areas of criminal law, teacher training, police training and memorials. In my view, there is now greater public awareness of the issue in Germany.

That is encouraging, because, just as in our personal lives, only when we as a society perceive a problem, are we also able to solve it. It has been a special experience for me to have these concerns heard and enforced politically.

The commitment against discrimination, racism and anti-Semitism has become, both professionally and personally, very important to me. I appreciate that important foundations for this were laid during my time in Duino. There I experienced how the coexistence of completely different people from all over the world can succeed, whilst having a lot of fun and forging friendships that last to this day.

I remember those responsible for the college at the time with gratitude and respect. David Sutcliffe was the central figure who had a profound impact on me, as he had on many others. He played a significant role in the success of the UWC in Duino and the entire UWC movement. His passing fills me with great sadness.

* Felix Klein
UWCAD 85-87 (student)
Native German
Felix is currently working as anti-Semitism Commissioner of Germany
Living in Berlin/Germany

Marc Glorius

Vino di Duino

Duino in slovene: Devin
Devin en français: Devine
auf Deutsch:
Finde des Rätsels Lösung
– errate! –
in italiano:
Smettetela di errare,
tornate a casa
Duino
divino
Hic!

2010

* *see further up*

Manuel Fernandez

Ten days ago I had a phone call ...

It deeply saddens me to have to write this note. It is now over twelve years since I last had something to do with the social service programme in the college I used to work... and yet I had this phone call.

For those of my friends unfamiliar with that college I can say in a nutshell that it used to be a wondrous pedagogical and formative experience; not only for the students but also for the teachers. It was a profoundly human experience of sharing life together between teachers arrived from many places (11 countries in my times) and just 200 students coming from over 80 countries. Everything that happened in the college – and so many things did happen – were run by teachers: all sorts of activities, drama productions, Carso days, Art "annuali", Conferences, International Affairs sessions, caving, climbing, skiing and whatever else might have caught the interest of a teacher and the alert and smart curiosity of a group of students.

I was somewhat amused at the interview when I originally applied for my post. The questioning was not as much about my knowledge of Economics but rather about what else I was able to offer. My UNICEF diploma as a leader of international voluntary work camps, which I had casually added to my application, received more attention than my PhD thesis and I was questioned about the nature of the work camps in which I had participated. I then took up the job in Duino and found every colleague involved in a vast array of endeavours totally unconnected with their academic subject. When I realised this buzzing activity, not without some dread I asked a colleague (who also was from a less developed country): "Listen, you already worked at one of these colleges. Do we actually have to do more than just teaching your subject?" His reply was "Yes, you have to give the hell out of you but then, you will have your long summer holiday."

So I joined my colleague David, from New Zealand, and we both ran the social service programme. David was unhappy with the pay and went back to his country. I then took full care of social service and did so for over 15 years. All students and all teachers participated in the social service programme, including the headmaster who, in all those years, took care of one of the most demanding services: an institution for severely mentally handicapped children and youngsters in the village of Medea. I remember how proud he was when he brought to our common room a newspaper that the children had produced.

Memories of that rich human experience flood my mind at this moment. I remember an evening when a student came to my house at the Palazzina and told me with some anxiety: "My roommate Marc has not come back from his social service; he was not there at dinner and he has not come to the room at all." I told him to be alert and come and tell me once Marc had come back." He did come back with a worried face at about 11 p.m. to confirm that Marc had yet not returned. It was about midnight when Marc appeared at my door and told me what had happened: he had gone to his service with signora Dora as usual that Tuesday. On previous Tuesdays he had thoroughly cleaned the balcony at the tiny old flat where Dora lived. On another Tuesday he had swept her chimney. Mark had been very busy engaged in long conversations with Dora who, after her experience at a Nazi concentration camp had become embittered against mankind while Marc tried his best to bring at least a shred of optimism.

There he was then, at my door, telling me what had happened: he had arrived to Dora's flat at S. Giacomo in Trieste, had entered and found Dora on the ground in great pain. She had fallen. Marc had called the ambulance and, when it came, he had accompanied Dora to hospital where she was interned with a severe fracture in her hip. In her pain Dora told Marc "My sister has to be informed." Marc took the address and navigated himself with the unknown transport system in Trieste and did manage to locate where the sister lived. When that task was completed it was already late in the night and he looked tired there at my place. "Did you have dinner Marc? Can I offer you something to eat?" "No, he said. I'm alright." Indeed, Marc was alright in a deeper sense: he was alright as a fellow and caring human being.

But I had that phone call …

I remember also Shemso and Sanja, both in my tutorial group and both enraged with reciprocal hatred when they had arrived to Duino. Sanja from Banja Luca had seen her mother dying during the Bosnian war and Shemso had seen his brother killed in Srebrenica in the same war but on opposite sides. They never ceased to ruminate about the evilness of the other but trough their common social service they learned to know one another and, still keeping their strong views, they exercised their tolerance in the practice of service to a third person.

I remember Paola telling me once: "Chatting with my social service it turned out that her family originates from Rovigno, which is where I live. She has never been to Rovigno afterwards so my parents will come this weekend and we shall take her with us to visit together my village." And so they did.

How can I not remember the commitment for service shown by everyone in the college – members of the administration included – when we worked in the refugee camps during the Bosnian war? (Particularly in the camp of Kozina that we had adopted.) And the experience with Lilia, the blind lady that became our Braille teacher?

Much closer to Duino, at Sistiana there was a charming elderly lady appropriately called signora Dolce. She was very weak and could hardly walk. One day the girls in her social service and Ximena knocked at her door to invite her to the Italian B drama production prepared by our students. Signora Dolce replied with some annoyance: "Ma già sapete che non posso camminare. Da due anni non ho fatto che uscire al negozio (25 m. away) una o due volte alla settimana e niente di più. Io non posso!" Yes, we know signora Dolce, the girls replied. But we shall come on Friday and take you to see this play." Still more annoyed Signora Dolce retorted: "No. Vi prego di non venire. Io non posso più muovermi di casa!" And there she remained, staring at them with an angry face. That Friday Ximena and the girls arrived at her place, knocked at the door and there she was. She had got her hair done and was dressing a beautiful robe, ready to come to our play. That is the meaning of stretching human beings to their full potential!

The task of coordinating social service did not prevent me from teaching my Economics classes and it drained away part of my holidays as the whole month of June had to be devoted to organizing the work for the next academic year, contact all institutions, make an evaluation of the work done, write letters of thanks to every outside person involved and, particularly, to sort out the forms from all first year students in which they expressed their preferences for service in their second year and have all of them fully allocated for a swift start of the social service programme immediately on the second week of the term. Then, as they arrived, the first years had social service introduced, mainly by second year students, and proceeded to choose their own service. All of this is documented on the archive I left in the College.

It was overall a very rich formative experience and maybe I should still devote time to write about it at greater length. I still keep, for example, the tapes with the long and amazing interviews we did to Anna Bonnacci. Many ex-students will remember her as in the last decades of the 102 years she lived she met students from many generations, from the very first one in 1982 to 2001. I keep also the Diploma of Honour given to us by the Red Cross for our services during the Bosnian War and the Diploma awarded to us by the Association of the Blind for the services to them.

All these experiences do touch you into the deepest cords of your heart. Students at their youthful and idealistic age always have an innate predisposition to express their built-in ethic of service and human solidarity and that was the beauty of being the coordinator of that important part of the college life. Nobody had to push them to that task. At times a student used to casually tell me "Manuel, I'm not going to social service today. I have a very demanding test tomorrow. I arranged with my lady to meet this Saturday and we shall cook lunch together." Of course that was fine. All I had to do was to see how a rapport was developed between students and their services. Once that strong human bond was created there was nothing much else to do. Students had got to own their services and normally did much more than what was expected. I would still be able to add almost countless instances of this experience that also enriched my life.

But I had that phone call …

In recent years, not long ago, progressively the college began to sort of "privatize" social service. The responsibility of coordinating the service was removed from teachers and was contracted out to an external officer who undertook the formal administration of this and made sure that students did fulfil this "duty". The coordination of the social service programme became an alien attachment to the life of the college and disconnected from the formative educational experience that is within the realm of teachers. Maybe that's better, more efficient and professional. Maybe …

But I did have that phone call …

It was ten days ago, when October of 2015 had arrived and the call came from one of the most cherished social services that we started

1991. The lady on the phone told me "Non so cosa succede ma nessuno si è fatto vivo per il social service." (I do not know what happens but nobody has come to this social service). Last night, 11th October 2015, I learned that the social service programme in that college still had not started.

How can that be possible?

The college has undergone many spells of acute economic crisis and I always contended that it would never close because of financial difficulties. The college would close in these two circumstances, in my view:

1.   When it would become totally irrelevant and nobody in the outside world would notice its presence and its meaning

2.   When the nice people in our village (Duino) would continue with their evolution of sentiments about the college – moving from the old enthusiastic welcome they offered to us at the beginning to the relative indifference and occasional disdain that one can observe these days – maybe arriving later to the point of rejection when they could ask in the future: "Go away from our village. We do not want you here." I most sincerely hope that such a point will never be reached and at least ourselves with Ximena preserve and cherish our attachment to Duino that remains our village and shall ever be so. We got to know almost every folk here and we shall keep them ever as good friends.

But there was that phone call and the confirmation that till last night the social service programme has not come to exist in the first term. Maybe there will be excuses like

-    The officer that runs the service is not available

-    Its substitute has not yet arrived

-    We did not realize it would take so much to start it this year

But there cannot be a justifiable reason. There cannot be a reasonable motive for not having foreseen the problem and worked out a solution during the long summer holiday. There is no excuse for the new academic year to have started without putting on the agenda this tremendous emergency that social service was delayed and something had to be done IMMEDIATELY to organize the service and have a programme ready for the moment the students arrived. There is no excuse whatsoever for not having started the social service on due time.

My sad reflections during last sleepless night I had led me to this most distressing realization:

It is not that the person in charge was not here on time.

It is not the fact that somebody failed to anticipate this and prepare an alternative solution before the academic year started

It is not that a first staff meeting was not devoted to organize an interim solution and find a volunteer teacher (or teachers) to undertake the task of starting off the social service.

No. Nothing of that can be a substitute for the real explanation which is this one: What has happened suggests that **the ethic of service has been lost in that college**. The absence of that consciousness is the only explanation possible.

After coming to such realization I am only left to one unescapable and utterly sad conclusion: there is not a terminal economic crisis, not yet complete irrelevance, not a full rejection from the village community but, as far as I am concerned, the college is closed.

I shall keep my contact with some two or three colleagues that I always appreciated, shall preserve my affection for those thousands of students with whom we shared life together in the past and shall have in good regard all new students who come to Duino with dreams and who perhaps may not find the ways to develop them to their full potential. And I shall keep my social service, of course.

Manuel (2015)

Post Scriptum

I am very touched by the contributions shared on the comments to this note. I thank everyone, particularly Maria Canfora and Gastone Pagot, knowledgeable friends who were kind enough to share a little bit of the missing information and have confirmed the solid reasons for concern regarding social service.

Gastone has informed us that the previous social service officer has taken a long term leave in Japan and Maria has confirmed that the social service programme and the long standing commitments the college has in this regard did start, or are still starting very late this year.

I have been quite removed from the life of the college these last years, not wholly by my own decision, and the only and tiny connection I keep is my contact with one of the most cherished services we started in 1991 and in the course of my visits I have had occasionally a very pleasant opportunity to get to know and chat with some of the students involved in this service.

On taking my leave from this very worthwhile exchange of opinions I am still left with some sombre doubts. These are some of them:

Once it became known that the officer in charge of one of the most important features of the college was taking a long term leave, I have no reason to doubt that the college moved swiftly and undertook a thorough process of selection of a successor. I can understand that this might have been a very hard and time consuming process. Once the sorting of the numerous applications was completed (in these times of crisis there are hundreds of very able and gifted people keenly applying for similar positions and the college surely might have spent some considerable time in the preliminary process of short-listing), then after the interviews would have taken place and when finally the best qualified and most appropriate person was chosen,

1) Was the person selected invited to come to the college in order to overlap with the previous officer, be briefed on the tasks ahead, and introduced to persons and institutions she/he would have to deal with in the coming future?

2) If the expected normal course of events was not viable and a delay was envisaged for the resumption of such an important feature – fundamental I would say – for the mission of the college during the beginning of the new academic year, were urgent contingent measures taken in order to fill the gap and start the social service programme in earnest in the new academic year?

3) Still, if the above proved to be too overwhelming for current capabilities, did the college take the time and the courtesy of informing all persons and institutions involved that the social service would have a late start this year?

Concerns like the above moved me to think that, after all, there was the danger that social service could have been moved out from the fundamental priorities in the life of the college and that was the main reason for my sadness and concern. It was that perception which momentarily has moved me out from my retirement and returned to me the dormant care I kept and shall always keep for a tremendously valuable venture in which I invested the best of my capabilities with enormous professional and human satisfaction.

I now take my own leave with the confidence that it is true what kind Maria expressed and I do appreciate: teachers, she said "still value social service, that we teachers still try to create a programme that is varied and stimulating for our students by sharing our enthusiasm for the college with them inside and above all outside of the classroom."

I trust that this also will be the feeling of the new person taking care of social service and I sincerely wish her well. Students are born with a built-in conscientiousness of solidarity and worthy ideals and my trust is put particularly on them, despite the fact that I may not have the pleasure of meeting them.

Thanks again for all your contributions.

Manuel

Manuel Fernandez Canque
UWCAD 83-03 (teacher)
Native from Chile
Author
Manuel taught economics in Duino, created the social services of the school and was a central figure of the school.
He and his wife Ximena are for many students the personification of humanitas.
Currently living near Monfalcone (GO)/Italy

Yves Aka

I was among luckiest to have had the opportunity to stay at the college for three years as opposed to the usual two-year programme. In early September 1985, when I arrived in Duino, I was not even fifteen years old, while the normal age of a first-öyear student was sixteen. During these years, though I did not interact frequently with Mr Sutcliffe, I recall him as a strong leader with a human touch and his dedication to the UWC movement.

The same goes for other people who have put my life on totally different trajectory and shaped it along the way during my years at the college and beyond. I also fondly recall Ms Valerie Quinlivan, who stood as godmother for my first communion and a year later, Mr Corrado Belci for my confirmation.

Both being real pioneers of the UWC Adriatic together Mr Sutcliffe and others, but also they were people I often looked up for advice and direction. Especially Mr Belci with whom I closely kept in touch through the years during my university years and throughout the early stages of my professional career, until he passed away.

I cannot underline enough the radical changes that the college has had in the life of that young teenager from West Africa. The values that have been instilled in me there had influenced my entire life.

After completing my university degree in Italy, I was looking into going to business school in the USA; and my focus had been in the school I ended up going to: Thunderbird School of International Management in Arizona; a graduate school that pretty much mirrored many of the UWC values albeit with a business twist.

Similarly to the UWC, Thunderbird also has a vibrant alumni network. I am proud and lucky to be part of both. These set of values guide me to this very day in my professional career. I'm currently in Germany, at the headquarter of a leading European financial services company and my primary tasks consist in helping shape our strategy in Africa via opening new subsidiaries, steering them and taking part in enhancing the financial services sector in many countries on the African continent.

A heartfelt thank you to these great men and women who, to a certain extend, raised me during these three crucial years at the United World College of the Adriatic in Duino, Italy.

Yves Aka
UWCAD 85-88 (student)
Native from Ivory Coast
Currently working as Corporate Governance Manager at Allianz
Living in Rome/Italy

Hans Raimund

Postskripta aus Duino

1
Viel Ansprache habe ich hier nicht

Die Vögel fehlen mir
Auch die Hasen
Von Rehen ist hier kein Rede mehr
Außer auf den Speisekarten und den Straßenschildern im
Karst

2
Frühmorgens krähen auch hier die Hähne
Und heute fiel ein Eichhörnchen ein schwarzes Zerzaust
aus einem Baum
Auf den Asphalt direkt vor meine Füße

3
Unlängst spät abends bei Zitronendropsmond
Schauten mein Hund und ich einem Igel zu
Neben einer Mülltonne drin Katzen rumorten
Fraß er Papierschnitzel stumpfsinnig

4
Wasser gibt es hier im Überfluß
Es macht mir Angst
Steht der Wind richtig rieche ich es bis ins Haus

5

Und die Bora! Die ganze Nacht
Klappern die Fensterläden liegen
Morgens aus den Scharnieren gerissen in den Büschen
Wetterseitig blättert der Verputz von den Fassaden

6

Auf den Feldern steht noch der Mais vom Vorjahr
Staubig weiß raschelt im Wind
Wieder ist es zu spät
Die Äcker abzubrennen

Platz zu machen für Neues Heuriges

Postscripts from Duino

1
Not many people to talk to here

The birds I miss
The hares too
Deer are never mentioned any more
Except on menus and road signs on the Karst

2
Early in the morning the cockerels crow here too
And today a squirrel tumbled
Black and ruffled from a tree

Onto the asphalt at my feet

3
Late one evening not long ago beneath a lemon moon
My dog and I watched a hedgehog
Near a dust bin chewing paper scraps apathetically
While cats rattled inside

4
Water is abundant here
It frightens me
When the wind is right I smell it all the way home

5
And the Bora! All night
Window shutters are clattering
In the morning they lie unhinged in the bushes
Plaster crumbles away from the weathered walls

6
Last year's corn still occupies the land
Rustling white and dusty in the wind
It is too late again
To burn down the fields

To make room for the new fort his year's crop

see further up

Marc Glorius

2913 km – A journey into the heart of Europe

Km 0

When you tell a story of a journey people who listen often have difficulties to follow. They are not ready to do so. Either they are absorbed by their lives in their cities. Or by their relationships. Or by their family, health and work situations.

Then there are a lot of films, texts and photos for advertisement or (self)marketing purposes about journeys and beautiful moments. Those mostly follow the path of a scenario in which only the expected may happen.

The sensation, energy, ecstasy and love of a real moment that is happening may seem ephemera.

Where does the energy of the live moment go – with its insights and excitements?

What is it there for?

Narrative I am strongly convinced is one possible and very good way to keep the memory of a strong experience awake.

So I am writing about a project, a journey. A project that ends with this text. A project that started precisely at the moment when I read the post in which A., an old school mate, was looking for someone to fetch a hundred pairs of skis and boots somewhere in Switzerland and bring them to a school in Mostar/Bosnia.

A. has for philanthropic reasons co-founded this particular school in Bosnia some years ago. A school guided by the same principles of experiential pedagogy and peace-seeking that had guided the school we used to go to 30 years ago. Both schools were founded in great parts by the same person: David B. Sutcliffe.

The length of the itinerary calculated by "viamichelin.fr" was 2913 km. My co-equipier and me would have to pass 7 countries in 5 days. A. living in England, the skis being in Switzerland and the school in Bosnia. Even if the journey was European, its pivotal countries were no (respectively soon no) members of the European Community. On the other hand: Both Switzerland and Bosnia with their multi ethnical populations in a long tradition aren't they micro-european communities par excellence? One as the only European country that has managed not to get involved in any war since 700 years, the other being one of the latest European battlefields.

The fact that Bosnia is not member of the EU caused difficulties. No car rental company was ready to rent us a van to bring us there. Where to get a van from? Would we have had the same problem going to Norway? The right move was to ask a similar school in Freiburg if they could lend us one of their vans. This vehicle turned out to be just perfect for the journey. I love its name: Transformer.

On the way there and the way back we stopped over in Duino/Italy which is midway between Mostar and Freiburg and the place of the United World College of the Adriatic, the school where A. and me used to go to. So the key to the solution was cooperation: Among schools: Robert Bosch College in Freiburg and the United World College in Mostar.

Among persons: Adriaan, Jale, Fleur, Ljubica, Mark, Laurence, Hannah, Anja, Corrado, Erfan, Sam, Mark and me.

It may be obvious, but still: The thing that is really interesting about live moments is that you are never sure of what is going to happen. You don't know whom are going to meet, how everything is going to look like, smell and feel. When you know the end of the book the adventure looses much of its thrill, of its uncertainty. Of its openness.

The definite yes for the Freiburg solution came only four days before the start of the journey. Getting to it involved many emails of half a dozen persons in concern. Interestingly enough the yes came just after me and my co-equipier had designed an alternative solution which consisted in renting a van, driving it until the Bosnian boarder and letting the skis get fetched by a van from Mostar. Thus renouncing to get to know country, town and school. I had already made a reservation at the car rental company. I was so happy when I canceled it!

To build the journey into an agenda of work and family duties felt like densifying an already dense area. Like implementing a new tooth. Facing the problem with the van I tried to contact A. He did not reply. I finally got a mail of his wife telling me that A. had had an accident burning himself on a bonfire and that she was taking over from him from now on.

Unpredictable events can happen while putting words into practice ...

Still: The element of fire is a central connect underlying the issue of the journey: Fire of the sun and its burning heat, fire of passion, fire of commitment, fire in the energy of the school project, fire in enabling a future but also fire of the bombs and the bullets destroying the city, killing many lives.

Km 257

The "5 stars" ski resort was high up in the mountains of Switzerland. It took many many serpentines to join it. Some hundred bikers made us company. They went to a convention. On a saturday in late summer. Beautiful and sunny.

When I entered the ski rental place (with integrated fashion and mountain bike shop plus an exclusive bar) I was surprised to hear the "Violent Femmes", Blister in the sun. A song that used to be a hymn of school days, rarely played nowadays and definitely rather grunge than posh.

Km 1458

33 hours, 8 coffees and 3 countries later, already very much in the South East of Europe: How easy would it be to cross the Croatian-Bosnian boarder? Although equipped with all kinds of papers the question was there. The boarder looked like we had imagined it: Huge. Scary.

It had been a while since I had seen such a boarder. Almost 30 years. Passing the communist part of Germany heading to Poland. Was it because it was late? Was it because of the blanket we had torn over the skis and the boots? Or just because we happened to pass in the right moment? The costumers were involved in a discussion.

They didn't even notice us.

Km 1556

I had been to Bosnia once, 1987, Yugoslavia still was there. Now my co-equipier and me were surprised to see ruins in the centre of Mostar. How present war still is in Mostar!

Its memory is everywhere in town. The monuments and ruins, less direct: the inscriptions on many houses saying who reconstructed them: The Germans, the French, the Italians. Present as discussion topic among people. Present in the atmosphere.

The historical centre of Mostar – never mind the many tourists – is of amazing beauty. The old bridge touches me like a song. An agent of truth. The panorama of the old town: A poem. Here we are sitting on the terrace of some restaurant with two wonderful teachers of the school. L. and H. are Bosnians. They teach German respectively French. They learned these languages during war. In France and Germany. Where they happened to stay during these years – 11 years old.

We can see the bridge from the terrace. We talk about symbols: Is their meaning made up by marketing and propaganda specialists? Or do they actually carry a (somehow) universal meaning from within? L. – fed up with propaganda of all different kinds – is skeptical about the latter. Me instead I advance some arguments for it.

Around midnight the day before we had arrived to Mostar. It had taken some effort to find our place to stay, "Anja and Vanja". A guy from a service station had been very helpful to us, making several calls on his cell phone – although we did not speak any language in common. Earlier today we had delivered the skis and visited the school. It is covering the second floor of a huge, old, reconstructed, yellow-orange building in the centre of the city.

The two floors underneath are taken by a croatian-catholic and bosniak school. These schools neither cooperate nor communicate with each other. The United World College on the second floor instead is trying to bring the world together by learning and practicing international understanding. It is offering an integrative education for 180 students from all over the world doing the International Baccalaureate (IB) in a two years course on scholarship base. One third of the students are coming from former Yugoslavia. All of them are living together in several residences spread over town. In contrast to the international "service" schools growing like mushrooms anywhere on earth intended to satisfy the needs of globally acting elites and gated communities the United World Colleges are schools with a "mission". The want to foster peace. Deeply influenced by Kurt Hahn's experiential pedagogy their school programme includes esthetical and physical activities, projects and social service. And an extraordinary experience.

Even among the UWCs the school in Mostar is outstanding. It is particular to this school that it is taking care of the local and regional contexts in which it is located while offering an international education. Most of the teachers are bosnian. Its facilities are humble (compared to the colleges in Freiburg or Duino). The purpose though is highly tangible: reconciliation. To build – within a divided community – an organism that is trying to live connectedness. Connectedness to the place, connectedness to one's roots, connectedness to world as a whole – thus bridging the local, the national and the international and melting it into one. Flower of peace on mined territory!

Mostar is a small city. With one "bulevar" (where the school building is located), several churches and mosques and many bars. From E. we hear a lot about the pre-war Mostar micro-culture. He describes it as a tiny "heart-warming", joke-making melting pot. Where one family could have different origins and where it did not matter if you or your neighbor were of muslim, serb or catholic-croatian origin. Where of all differences a unique urban culture had melted. We meet E. while he is immersed singing a sentimental song at full voice with the other clients of a café-bar. At two o'clock in the afternoon! He later joins us on the terrace where we are having coffee. And he starts telling us about Mostar, how it used to be before war, how he used to jump from the 22 meters high bridge, how he left for Germany, how he has been coming back here since then remembering the beautiful days. Now crying over the ruins. He invites us for lunch. He is looking to the sky repeating that he does not understand, that he cannot understand. He ends up claiming: "The nationalists, fascists, extremists have had their five minutes", then looking deeply in our eyes: "When are we going to have ours?"

Km 2706

On the way back for some reason the Gotthard-tunnel is closed. We have to pass the mountain. Heavy rain, an infinite amount of construction sites and of tunnels … From the 7 European countries we passed through the most challenging one was Switzerland, presumedly an island of safety.

Km 2913

We arrive home just before the rise of the day. I have breakfast, coffee and go to work.

Two days later something strange occurs to me. On a walk through the forest: . At the bottom of a hill some hundred meters ahead I see two dogs. One is seeming upset. The situation feels weird. While coming nearer I realize that there are two ladies with them. One is talking on her cell phone. The other is holding her dog that is strongly attracted by something that I thought being the other dog. Actually it is the back of a horse – colored brown – lying there. "What happened to the horse?" I ask the lady. "It's dead", she answers, "it just died."

I wouldn't be able to explain why, but I had a similar feeling in Mostar seeing the traces of war.

PS

The "landscape" of the city of Mostar seems fairly far away from the "landscape" of the city of Basel (nearby I live). Memorised from here Mostar almost seems unreal. War does not even seem to be an option of thought in Switzerland. Future is definitely assumed to happen peacefully. Everything is built into it.

In my hometown Cologne/Germany "post war memory" instead is still present .

Almost completely destroyed during World War II the pain and the wounds caused at this occasion are somehow still tangible today.

L. tells us that Mostar until some years ago used to be the "playground" of all sorts of anarchists, idealists and artists arriving from all over Europe. They came with many many ideas about how to change it, how to make it better, how to make it work. Usually they left quite fast disappointed that reality wouldn't keep up with their ideas and dreams.

I also feel the place inspirational. Actually it is difficult for me to speak about it. Nothing left me indifferent. A ruin has an openness. It is somehow inviting future to manifest.

I definitely like open places. Usually they carry some wounds with them.

It is a myth though that you need war to create them. That is simply not true. People who believe that, are definitely mixing up heaven with hell.

A koan comes to my mind: A zen-pupil is complaining: "I spend all my time working in my garden. Every time it is finished my master comes and throws a huge stone into it."

Places I feel open I call them "3 star". Connected to different realities and perspectives. Part of an open narrative. Constantly creating and recreating themselves, with non-defined areas. Wild flowers grow there. Where you feel the heart. The blood. The soul. Places striving for unity. Inclusiveness. The school in Mostar I felt like this. Maybe also the town.

The persons we met, the hot wind, the burning sun, the ruins, also of Pan-Yugoslavia, the stony hills around, nothing left us indifferent. The city feels hurt. The school has a dream. My impression is: The keys of a European union are kept here.

(Autumn 2018)

Cornelia Vospernik

As I am writing this, I am at a table brought from China, in a place bought in Trieste, reposing a few days from my job as ORF bureau chief in Rome. And it kind of tells it all. Since I first set my sight on this sea that seemed to be infinite to the young girl from the mountainous country, since I first left home at the age of 16, I always wanted to do two things: travel the world first and come back to Trieste then. I think, I am about to come full circle.

When I was a teenager, I idealised this place as an escape. Now it is a true coming home. What came in between has foundations in years I cannot marvel to look back at now. How young we were! How unexperienced! How naïve in this world without the internet, mobile phones, globalization. We needed a "permesso di soggiorno" to even be here. Travel then was a real adventure. And it took forever. There were borders, blocks and atomic disasters looming over us. We lived in a time nobody knew which of the two sides would press the button first. Our world seemed binary. And so easy for that matter. Yet, it was not. Us, bunch from all over the world learned long before so many had the chance to "befriend" virtually everybody, and I mean, virtually, what it meant to face the people inhabiting this world.

We had the world in the Foresteria. We had to learn to handle our preconceptions, lack of knowledge, stupidity. We did so by facing each other. And befriending each other. And growing with each other. The friends I made in the College are the deepest friendships I have. I mean deepest in the sense of how we know and accept each other. How there is not even a hint of trying or having to pretend.

And how it is of no interest to any one of us who made what of their lives, because whenever we meet, we are the same young bunch. I had this exchange the other day with a year mate, and I will not tell, whom, who sprained his ankle while bringing the garbage to the bin. He was complaining of a silly swollen ankle even though he was not climbing Everest. Well, I replied. We are getting old. Garbage bins are our Everests now, but the sky is still our limit.

I admit, it took time, to fully gauge the lasting effects the UWC had on me. There was an immediate effect, of course. I would not have gotten into reporting foreign countries without this experience. My professional life was laid out in 1986 when I stepped into Duino, I think. Other effects were subtler. I don't know how it is or was for others, but I guess for many of us the 20th and most of the 30th were spent aiming higher and away, without knowing, where to. And then we found each other again, on this subtle way I mentioned.

There is an unique experience connecting us. It is more than the countless tea cups and Muratti's spent discussing life or love pains on the floor of the entrance to Foresteria, more than trying to figure out what will be asked when in the IB, more than one line of Rilke understood and yelled out in class, and more than the first sangria you ever had in your life and how sick you felt, even more than covering for your roommates or hitchhiking to the Cote D'Azur.

These are just stories probably no teenager today would understand. And no parent would accept. Ours, luckily, didn't know about it. We were a special breed. And I think we are connected by something like a special code. I met people from different generations and colleges back in Austria but we all connected on this unspoken UWC code, no matter if we were Duino 86-88, Wales in the 70th or Pearson's in the late 90th.

Now I am back in this Italy I know and love from the 80th, in a semi-lockdown in zona arancione, faced with an ugly side of globalization. More than ever before I feel trapped not being able to just go and see friends and yet consoled to get the chance to learn again that physical distance is just an outer layer. I don't know if this pandemic will bring the world closer together. But I am quite sure that us, UWC-breed of a certain generation, is better equipped to handle it. As to myself: I hope, my beloved Italy survives it, and I hope, my UWC Duinesi will make it back here. I definitely will. I have the last quarter of my circle already mapped out before me: A few more years as a journalist. And then I want to do yoga on Molo Audace, speak wonderful yoga nidra in Italian to people who never heard it and hike up to Duino once in a fortnight to give them these Rilke-sessions the German speakers there don't get any more.

After a lifetime of writing and reading I might as well teach another generation on the Rilke path to just spell it out. And to do so with the best their voices can give. I shall speak to them about the importance of the vishuddhi chakra and proper German pronounciation and how to lead their voice between upper and lower tones like an instrument, at the same time.

And then, I want to hear it from another generation, interpreted in their own voices:

"Wer, wenn ich schriee, hörte mich denn aus
der Engel Ordnungen " …

Because Duino is eternal on more than one level.

* *Cornelia Vospernik*

UWCAD 86-88 (student)
Native from Austria and Slovenia
Journalist, author and interpreter
Cornelia is renowned journalist at ORF (Austrian national television and radio)
She was correspondent in China, author of three books giving inside view of daily life there
Head of office of ORF in Italy
Currently living in Rome

Hans Raimund

IM SCHNEIDER

Ich fädle
Das Licht
Ins Augenöhr

Ich stichle
Die Finsternis
Mit Pupillennadeln

Ich säume
den Tag
mit Wimpernborten

Ich nähe
Falten
In die Nacht

Ich setz
Dem Leben
Zwickel ein

Der Tod
Sitzt mir
Wie angegossen

Infilo
La luce
In cruna d'occhio

Punzecchio
L'oscurità
Con aghi di pupille

Orlo
Il giorno
Con cimosa di ciglia

Cucio
Pieghe
Nella notte

Applico
Alla vita
Un rinforzo

La morte
Mi va
A pennello

see further up

*Each detail is important.
As important as the
whole picture*

(Frank Bodin)

III. Remembering David Sutcliffe - Tributes

Preface

The following chapter gathers the tributes published on the Facebook page "Remembering David Sutcliffe" created by Manuel Fernandez and others directly after his death in November 2019. The texts tell many different episodes in connection with David Sutcliffe, episodes that are important and essential for the contributors.

These are humorous, lovely, thoughtful sometimes painful memories and reflections that transmit an authentic feeling and draw a colorful picture. Something poetical emerges out of them, a vivid mosaic of the beginnings.

(1)

I am very grateful to the friends who made it to David's funeral, particularly with those who assured me that they were carrying my condolences as they knew that my good new friend, a Mr Parkinson, does not let me travel. I want to explain the cryptic reference to those two candles Cille lit at the Cathedral in Oslo.

It was early March in 1985 when at about 3:00 o'clock in the morning I was awaken by a long-distance phone call. It was from one of my brothers in Chile giving me the sad news of my mum's passing. There I remained, sitting on my bed and pondering about what I had to do. The College contract contained a clause with the provision of a week's permission for bereavement in such cases. Notwithstanding that possibility I considered, in the first place, what would my mum have desired for me to do on that morning. She was a humble indigenous woman from an Andean village who only had studied up to Primary three, but she always told us that she would have loved to be a teacher. So strong was her feeling that all her six children became teachers and as I was one of them, I felt that my duty on that morning was simply to carry on normally with my lessons. We did not tell this to anybody and I delivered my lessons as usual, maybe not quite as usual but I did carry on normally, also with my daily social service commitment.

When my last morning lesson was about to start on that same morning, Cille approached me quietly and requested permission to leave the class 10 minutes before the end. I noticed in her face that it would have been impossible for me to deny that request. She sat next to the door and quietly left the room at the time convened. And that was that.

Many years later, when we met again at a reunion, I asked Cille for the reason behind her request of permission. She told me then, with a face similar to that of the past, that on that day her beloved grandma had died and Cille's dad asked her not to come home for the funeral so as not to endanger her academic performance. That was the reason for her visible sorrow when she had requested those 10 minute's permissions. She told me that, although she was not a believer, she had entered Duino's chapel, lit a candle and sat down to reflect and mourn in silence. As she finished her explanation, I told Cille that on the very same morning I also had received a phone call informing about my mum's death.

"The candle you lit, therefore", I told her, "was not only for your grandma but also for my mum."

Afterwards lovely Cille has religiously continued lighting that candle year after year and I am at all times aware that, on that day, in faraway Oslo somebody has lit a candle in memory of that humble Andean Indian who was my mother. Cille now added another candle at Oslo Cathedral to enrich that memory with a remembrance of David B. Sutcliffe. That's the reason for the second candle and I feel comforted by what she has done, from a non-believer on behalf of another non believer. Thank you so much Cille. You made bearable my absence from David's funeral. [I had asked Cille's permission to tell this story.]

(2)

David B. Sutcliffe and the secret event – 1994

It was one day in mid-February 1994 when I went up to David's office and asked to see him for a couple of minutes. He allowed me to come in and I entered wearing a smile. I told him:

"David, I would like to prepare a secret event for the college."

Half intrigued he replied:

"And what is it?"

"Can't tell you. It is secret." I replied.

He looked at me with an amused expression and said; "Is there any cost involved"

"Yes", I replied, "500,000 lire" [Around 300 Euro nowadays]

Without much hesitation and keeping his smile on he replied: "Alright"

I'll shall always remember that moment and that expression, as if I had heard it then for the first time: All right!

At the next Monday assembly, I made the announcement that a secret event would take place on the evening of Friday the 4th of March at Palazzine Dayroom. Everyone looked intrigued. Then I asked for a volunteer to help and Pilvi instantly rose her hand. Then with Pilvi we started a colourful publicity campaign around the college for about ten days, increasing the expectation as the event was approaching. At a staff meeting I invited all colleagues to attend and neither to them a hint was released.

The event was planned thanks to the delightful complicity of Antonietta, an ex-student from Rome. The plan was to bring over an excellent group of Irish music: "The Kay McCarthy Ensemble." The group arrived on the evening prior to the event; tired and sleepy after the long trip from Rome in an old van. After partaking a dinner Ximena had prepared and engaging into a friendly and animated conversation, we hid the group in our garage, where we had improvised some rough beds that only their tiredness made bearable and they all entered into deep sleep.

While students were having their dinner the next day, with Pilvi and Ximena we set up the place with chairs and arranged the stage distributing on all seats copies of a songbook we had prepared. Kay had told us in advance the programme.

The intrigued public gathered outside Pala well before the start time and could only enter the dayroom when everything was set. Once everyone was inside, we asked to welcome the Kay McCarthy Ensemble as they were entering the Dayroom from the shower area next to the kitchen. Once they had been welcomed, wonderful Kay then took over in such a professional and friendly manner that she immediately owned the place plus our admiration when old Palazzina walls began to tremble with her sweet and powerful voice, so well blended with the music of excellent performers. Very proud Antonietta, our ex-student, was also a member of the group. It was a marvellous evening and the group was deeply touched by the enthusiastic participation of the young audience.

And that was that.

One day, sometime after that event in Duino, a carefully wrapped parcel arrived from Rome. It contained "Aris", a CD with a brilliant rendering of a well-selected sample from the vast Irish musical treasure. It contained some of the pieces performed at Duino which I found so beautiful and familiar. There was also a letter the content of which thus comes to my recollection:

The ensemble, Kay wrote, had been somewhat at a low ebb before coming to Duino.

The ghost of disbandment was haunting all members. The group had produced two wonderful albums in 1978 and 1983 but nothing else during the following years. One of musicians in the ensemble had already found a position in the prestigious RAI Orchestra. They thought that the Duino experience would be, perhaps, their final farewell.

I want to think that the "secret event" experience, the full three days they spent closely together, the warmth and sheer enthusiasm of that juvenile audience might have led to a profound experience of reckoning with themselves. The fact was that after their arrival in Rome a firm decision had been agreed upon. The "Kay McCarthy Ensemble" was reinvigorated and a new era of increasing success was begun.

At the end of the letter Kay explained that the enclosed album – "Aris" – was the first result of their renewed experience and, "to a large extent," she added "there is so much of you in this CD and in our new beginning". "You" of course meant the college, that charming crowd of rascals clapping, singing and inserting themselves into that joyful performance.

The Kay McCarthy Ensemble was restarted with great success with numberless tours and thousands of albums sold. They became "an icon of Irish music made in Italy" as a critic wrote.

So, the secret event was all right, the students were all right, the performers were all right; fundamentally, everything was the result of the initial "all right" pronounced by you David, and in mysterious ways, unwittingly, you changed also the lives of people who were not our students; lives that changed, to use a memorable Italian expression, "alla tua insaputa".

Thank you, David, for your life also was all right and much more than all right. When I posted my note on the "Secret event" I should have added a warm message sent by Kay McCarthy With my excuses I am adding it now.

....

Grazie di avermi scritto. Antonietta mi aveva già informata della morte di David Sutcliffe, una delle persone più belle che abbia mai conosciuto – *He had all the "gentleman-becoming graces"*. Con questa morte un'altra tessera del mosaico delle mie conoscenze si è trasformata. Ma non si è spenta. È strano che la memoria di una persona con la quale avrò scambiato cento parole in tutto sia rimasta così viva, meravigliata e colma di rispettoso affetto! Credo che la forza dello spessore umano di David Sutcliffe emanasse spontaneamente da tutta la sua persona. Ecco cosa intendevo con "*gentleman-becoming graces*".

C'eravamo conosciuti durante "l'*infanzia*" dell'UWCAD – quattro o cinque anni prima che Antonietta diventasse una "collegina" – quando venni a Duino per dare lezioni di lingua irlandese ad una studentessa irlandese, Dara McClatchie.

In quei pochissimi giorni ospitata al Motel Agip, capii che il collegio e Sutcliffe erano un uno simbiotico. Il fatto che il suo cognome facesse rima con Heathcliff mi faceva sorridere come sto sorridendo mentre ti scrivo. Per colpa di questa assonanza devo sempre ricordarmi di non aggiungere una "h" dopo la "t" di Sutcliffe. Strani scherzi del flusso della coscienza! Cosa avevano in comune David Sutcliffe con il terribile protagonista di Wuthering Heights? La passione, credo, ma manifesta in due modi opposti sullo spettro della razionalità.

...

Il resoconto di Manuel del nostro concerto a "sorpresa" mi onora. Come ho detto prima, la tessera del mosaico delle mie esperienze che reca il nome di David Sutcliffe è cambiato. Non è scomparsa, però. Ha solo subito un "*sea change*", illuminandosi "d'immenso".

Un abbraccio.

....

(3)

Dear David –

It is perhaps the greatest test, of the very principles that you led your life so passionately, dedicatedly, courageously, and with such extraordinary focus and stamina to champion and to embody in your work building the UWC movement and thus your service to these very principles.

Principles of a fearless challenge to status quos that must be changed in order to benefit the greater good, Principles of the courage to speak the truth, even if it be unpalatable to the many who do not wish to hear it –

Principles of *integrity*, above all, and of putting the good of the many above the consequence to self, where needed –

that I find myself in front of my keyboard right now, writing this from my heart to yours, tied in a knot.

As over the past four days I have quietly witnessed accolade after heartfelt accolade pour into here from every corner of the globe, from the countless people whose lives you have touched so deeply ...

And this test of these principles to which I refer has therefore been:

Do I speak up?

Do I tell my story?

Deeply personal testimonies, that have been in such contrast to my own personal experience of you during my two years as a student at UWCAD with you as my headmaster and teacher in charge of our windsurfing activity, where we hardly spoke a word to each other, week after week after week.

Do I dare to exercise my right to challenge the status quo here in this group, the same right and privilege and responsibility I invoke every day in my life's work of being a leadership coach and facilitator, fighting on the front lines of reducing gender and diversity inequality, promoting inclusion and belonging, bringing critical life skills to young people and the workplace, to improve their mental health and enable them to thrive through adversity, and fulfil their true potential –

A choice I have consciously made to dedicate myself to, as an explicit pay-it-forward and demonstration of gratitude for my time at UWC, my personal lifelong way of honouring the principles it embodied, that you embodied ...

And tell a contrary tale here, of how searing your last words to me were, how long the shadow they threw over my self-worth, because –

This, too, is an equally solid fragment of the whole truth?

And, in this the final reckoning of your life's impact, that in the flood of grief and gratitude so richly-earned, there should also be a seat at the table for those of us who experienced something other than the kindness and care and nurturing that the vast majority have received from you?

David, I write these words carefully because I want to honour your spirit of integrity by giving a voice to these "other voices", which normally under such circumstances would ordinarily be held respectfully silent.

"Let bygones be bygones," we say. "People are human." You had an exceptionally tough remit, being Papa' to such a group that was us, and generations upon generations before and after.

But –

We were taught, in the schools you created.

TOK: question "how we know what we know?" "What is our basis of what we take as 'truth'?" "How do we arrive at our judgments?"

I believe your answer to this would be an unequivocal Yes.

Even if that subject of examination is ... your own life and legacy. Because I believe you are that extraordinary a man.

And you would see this in its proper light –

– My story's pretty simple, really.

And – if we are to go on with the good and worthy work that I believe you want us to do after our time at UWC,

Must we not also take the same critical, objective lens to ourselves? Our own leaders? Our own institutions?

that this careful, nuanced, critical, compassionate scrutiny in itself is a resounding vote of confidence in, a living embodiment of, the very educational and life principles you wanted UWC to install in every single one of us.

At the end of my last term at Duino, spring 1996, you left me and my parents these words as your parting shot in my final school report.

The sting remains so undiminished after 23 years that even as I extracted my report two days ago from the clear plastic folder in which I have kept it, stashed in an overlooked corner of my cupboard, and forced myself to run my eye through your words again ...

The tears still rise. Along with the stab in my heart.

As they have faithfully done so each time I have brought myself to read them, from the very beginning when I first read it as a vulnerable, stressed, overwhelmed and unsupported 18-year-old, returning to a family in Singapore that had been falling apart during the two years of my absence, and for which this pronouncement from my headmaster was to cause yet more pain and confusion and recrimination.

For you had written from the position of your responsibility. You were my headmaster. This was my capstone, a chance to review my time at the college, and all that I had in my flawed, sincere way, striven to give. And you gave your judgment.

It did not matter that your colleagues had written consistently and positively about my efforts in other areas of college life.

You had felt strongly enough that I had let you down, bitterly enough to merit the words, "questions naturally arise about the level of her seriousness and commitment when hard work is called for."

"She has thrown away an opportunity ... simply through lack of application."

"My own belief is that she should reflect very carefully on her performance at the College which has been acceptable but could have been outstanding. Why such a waste?"

As the stress piled up with EE deadlines, college and scholarship applications, personal life challenges, and I started to crumble, what that seemed to say to you was: Yee Leng was just not applying herself.

It's her responsibility that she mucked up what could have been a stellar performance during her time here.

The fault was, in your opinion, wholly and completely mine. These didn't seem to matter to you. Not really.

———

And why she is behaving this way, what could be some root causes, what could have been done to understand and support ...

I sometimes wonder what you might have written instead, had you known what the IB examining board would return a month later.

That the same individual whom you castigated for her "lack of seriousness and commitment when hard work is called for" would end up delivering the College its second-highest IB score in that year: 43, with 4 Highers taken instead of the usual 3, every single one a 7.

Who proceeded to earn a full scholarship to Oxford, and with her time at Duino practicing on her own while she could at the Accademia, teaching herself pieces the Trio had no time to teach her and performing those at recital for her fellow students of her own accord, went on to win the Instrumental Scholarship as the only non-music major her college had bestowed the scholarship on.

———

These didn't matter, not really.

Because the damage to her sense of self had already been internalised.

I have spent much of the slow two and a half decades since 1996 learning how to be grateful for the gift you gave me through my cool, distant, and yes – on occasion, harsh – interactions with you, David.

For I would not be caring as passionately as I do now about young people's psychological wellbeing, and taking it upon myself to work with educational institutions, organizations, teams, and individuals to help people understand their own shortcomings, be kind and caring to themselves and to others, and to grow into their fullest potentials.

I would not have become an interculturalist, fascinated by the way cultures and groupthink, behaviours and norms can be seeded and propagated, for good and for ill, for liberation and for oppression, for hero-making and for iconoclasm, for myth-creating and story-retelling.

For the cult of UWC is a strong one. A good one, in so many ways. And this scrutiny must be a fundamentally democratic one –

———

And so –

So do I here, in a deep, distilled spirit of gratitude and appreciation of all the

But one that, precisely because it is so powerful, precisely because it holds such thrall over us who have been forever changed through traversing its portals, I argue requires the exact same standards of sober, objective scrutiny of its whole, as we ourselves had been trained to apply on everything we studied during our time there, and since.

One that allows each and every one of us who has a voice and a personal experience, to share that experience, plainly and honestly, without shame or guilt or fear.

As I teach in my intercultural workshops the old Indian story of the blind men and the elephant, each of whom perceives but a part of the greater truth ...

greatness of man that you were, even with moments I personally found profoundly regrettable, such as the above ... so do I offer my little story here, to sit alongside the hundreds and thousands of others as a collective constellation of the giant of a human being that you were.

And I choose here to do so, in a spirit of clear-eyed, clean-hearted, warm celebration.

That through it all, even with me, in your own way you _cared_. You really did. Otherwise you wouldn't have done what you did, as destructive as it may have been for me back then. And it was.

I can see this now. I can understand, and hold space, for it now. And from my heart to yours –

I thank you for it.

In love and peace, and warmth,

Y.L.

(4)

If you wondered why sometimes DBS came across as stern and un-approachable, the family tribute by his daughter Veronica shed some light on aspects of his developments as a child that you may also not have been aware of:

1. Having moved to Guernsey at the age of 3 with his family, DBS and his mother and siblings were evacuated in 1940 when the Nazis occupied the island. He did not get to see his doctor father again until 1945, as he stayed behind and suffered the German occupation for 5 years.

2. When David fell in love with Elisabeth at Salem (where his UWC journey started) and got married to her in Tübingen, his parents refused to attend the wedding to a German.

3. In 1947, only aged 13, DAVID was sent off to a tough boarding school.

4. Years later in a radio interview his father admitted that Elisabeth was the best possible wife he could have wished for his son.

(5)

Oh boy, DBS has passed away. I remember him most from a single meeting he had with my parents and me. My parents had unexpectedly come to visit the college to tell me my mother was dying of ALS. They had given David notice of this. He asked us in for a meeting the morning after they broke the news and he spoke with such humanity about the loss of his son a few years before and what such a loss does to people. That moment, the stern and distant headmaster became a vulnerable human being and it touched me deeply. He was so kind after that.
I know he could be harsh when crossed, but I just remember him with tears in his eyes, trying to help us when we needed it.

(6)

Thank you DBS for your leadership. Thank you for your personal encouragement, and showing that you believed in us students. I still recall your personal notes in the report cards. We carried that with us, long after we left AC. My thoughts are with you Elizabeth, Veronica and Michael. I was fortunate to spend good times with you Michael in AC in 78-80, and traveling around Europe during the summer thereafter. I hope you can find solace in that your Dad positively influenced the lives of so many people.

(7)

Ever since Mr Fernandez gave us the devastating news, Mr and Mrs Sutcliffe and my time at AD in 1986-88 have been constantly on my mind, even in my sleep. Some memories surfaced immediately, whereas others I have had to dig a little deeper to find.

Mr Sutcliffe was not somebody I would ever dare to strike up a casual conversation with in the streets of Duino, but he was still omnipresent in our every day life. My first proper meeting with him happened in the midst of a crisis. Upon our return from the opening of the academic year in Rome in my first year, I received a telephone call from my mother during supper at Agip telling me my grandmother had suddenly and completely unexpectedly died while I had been away. I went into an immediate state of shock and didn't get a wink of sleep that night.

The next morning I called in sick with the nurse and went straight to Mr Sutcliffe's office and asked to talk to him. I don't think I had to wait long before I was admitted. I then poured my heart out to him and asked for permission to leave early for Christmas in order to be with my family in the time of mourning. It was immediately granted with no ifs and buts, for which I will be eternally grateful. Upon returning from my extended holiday, I joined Mrs Sutcliffe and (if I recall correctly) her daughter Veronica along with a couple of ex students on a visit to the Anglican church in Trieste for a service celebrating the Epiphany on 6th January. It is actually one of my fondest memories from the college.

Where Mr Sutcliffe was awe striking, Mrs Sutcliffe was a lot more approachable and always very friendly. And yet, when reading my annual report cards, Mr Sutcliffe's final comments about me were strikingly to the point and made me realize just how much he had actually observed from a distance and really understood. Several years later, when I learnt of Edward's passing away, just as suddenly and seemingly out of the blue as the death of my own grandmother, it had a great effect on me as people our age (twenties) were not supposed to die and especially not somebody I knew. I was initially terrified of intruding on Mr and Mrs Sutcliffe during such a hard time, but luckily I overcame my intimidation and finally wrote them a letter of condolences asking some confused questions about what on earth had happened.

O my pleasant surprise: Mrs Sutcliffe soon wrote me a long letter back, taking her time to explain to me in detail what they knew so far about her son's mysterious death. I was immensely relieved that my letter had not been seen as an intrusion, but rather the contrary, and very grateful that Mrs Sutcliffe would actually take her time to address my concerns, that she opened up for me to share in her grief even though I had never been a personal friend of Edward's.

I realised already then that the loss of their youngest child must have been devastating for them, but now as I have become older and wiser it has dawned upon me even more how hard it must have been for them to carry on with their work after such a mind blowing loss.

(8)

Today my thoughts are with David Sutcliffe and his family. All my respect for a great man that meant so much for United World College and everyone involved in the movement. We need people like him to stand up for international understanding more than ever. His legacy is a reminder for all of us who believe in openness and tolerance to work harder and do more.

(9)

Despite technologies connecting people globally, today the UWC mission is ever relevant as discrimination, popularism and disregard for our natural resources is on the rise, in so many places. Mr Sutcliffe embodied and dedicated his entire life to structural changes in a personalised way that set all of us on our own path, and a different one because of him.

To that I am eternally grateful. May he Rest In Peace.

(10)

When I was interviewed for the regional selections in Duino, David asked me where would I go if he gave me a blank air ticket. I surprised myself (and possibly him) by replying "China", a country whose culture and traditions had always fascinated me. Little did I know that about thirty years later I would be supervising dozens of Chinese PhD students and that I would visit China 6-8 times a year.

During my two years in Duino David never ceased to surprise me. Whenever he made a controversial decision, I would always express disagreement with him (a couple of times even in person, I believe). Yet as soon as I calmed down and stopped to think over the whole situation, I would end up realizing that in his shoes, I would not have been able to do any better, or any different.

In addition to his huge personal contribution to the Colleges, David deserves credit also for choosing the right people to work with. Any major effort like a UWC requires team work and he picked the best team members he could find.

On a couple of occasions, without knowing me particularly well, he put me in charge of a certain situation (not fully appreciating the kind of rascal I was, from time to time. Or maybe he did, and was hoping I would grow up. I will never know). The faith he placed in me surprised me and gave me confidence. Even if it happened only twice, it was a huge boost in self-esteem, which helped me immensely in growing up.

In hindsight he was an extremely wise and patient man. He handled multiples of 200 rowdy, insubordinate and horny teenagers with remarkable skill and composure.

Once we had a visit from Prince Charles and the whole College ended up attending a special concert at Teatro Verdi in Trieste. I was sitting in the front row on the stage and was the only one who refused to stand up for both the Italian and British hymns (one of my pet peeves ... I don't believe in national anthems, nor in fact in anything that emphasizes "nation", as opposed to "human"). I recall with a smile that another student (will not name names) did not stand up for the British anthem. Had I been in David's shoes I would not have reacted kindly to that kind of disrespect. And yet I barely got a mild scolding, if anything at all (my dad on the other lectured me profusely when I called home, as he was in the audience during the event and wanted to go hide).

We sometimes placed him in impossible situations and he always handled them with poise and equanimity.

He even had a very particular sense of humour.

I recall some of the words he said at the end of year speech in May 1990: "In my role as headmaster, I am often expected to see things I do not see, and not to see other things that I see quite well ..."

(11)

I found out only recently that David passed away and I never got to thank him properly for what he did for me. He was the head of the UWC committee in Albania in 2001 and was the one who saw potential in me and gave me the opportunity for a better future by awarding me the UWC scholarship. I went into the admissions process completely alone and without even updating my parents as I passed from round to round. It was a long shot and I expected to see preferential treatment towards other students whose families had connections, something I had grown used to seeing and experiencing as a growing teenager in Albania. I was surprised to find out that David was paying attention to me when I spoke in the group interviews. I felt he truly connected with me, and silently made me feel emboldened to give it my best shot. I felt that for once, I was going to get a fair chance at being evaluated.

Thanks to him, I ended up studying at the Red Cross Nordic United World college in Norway and building a life focused on passion and meaning, not constantly fighting the system. I'm forever grateful to David for this chance and appreciative for all the other lives that he changed by giving opportunities to kids who otherwise would have none.

Thank you David, forever touched by your gift .

(12)

The memorial act for David at Duino Church last Sunday went fine. There was a good crowd and we were honoured with the presence of Signora Maria Luisa Belci, daughter of Corrado Belci, plus Dr Maria Carmela Posarelli, the lady doctor who had served our students during David's times.

We were very grateful also for the presence of Irene Bidoli Poclen, widow of Maestro Piero, our treasured choirmaster at the Duino UWC during the period of its greatest splendour. Before leaving Irene left a donation for the Mostar College.

Although it was intended mainly for people from Duino there was a nice presence of some ex-students. Don Giorgio Giannini, the local priest, although now in retirement, kindly made all arrangements for this act of remembrance and opened the event by making very touching remarks on his personal friendship with David and then he left the meeting on my hands. Two ex-students read out pieces written by other ex-students to illustrate relevant parts of my address.

I was very pleased to remark to Duinese friends on the similarities between Duino and the tiny Fermain Bay in Guernsey, Channel Islands – where, according to some brief autobiographical notes written by David – he used to go out fishing with his dad when he was four (DBS: *"My first memory of being afloat on a small craft was on 3rd September*

1939. I was not quite five years old. My father, two of his friends and I were anchored in a small cabin cruiser, fishing in Guernsey's Fermain Bay"). Both bays, Fermain and Duino bear similarities but for the castles missing in the former.

At the end of the meeting the priest again made a remark on David's Christian beliefs and asked all who desired to join in the Lord's Prayer. I am not a believer but found that ending very appropriate and touching, as if all present were paying a tribute to David.

I would like to thank all those who attended and the numerous messages of support sent by people who were unable to attend.

Thanks Adelaide and Devan for reading out those pieces.

(13)

In memoria di David Sutcliffe, primo rettore del Collegio del Mondo Unito di Duino. Questo è un invito a ricordare il primo rettore del Collegio del Mondo Unito, un amico di Duino scomparso il giorno 11 novembre di questo 2019. A Duino rimarrà nella memoria il suo proposito di considerare il villaggio un luogo in cui il collegio si doveva inserire con umiltà e spirito di servizio.

Non ha voluto soltanto fare cose "per il villaggio", bensì "con il villaggio". Ad esempio:

-    Il servizio sociale volontario che i ragazzi hanno svolto per anni tenendo compagnia a numerosi anziani del villaggio.

-    Il progetto che instaurò con quasi tutti gli abitanti del paese, dove duecento famiglie duinesi avevano accolto nelle loro case uno studente del collegio ognuna.

Ogni ragazzo o ragazza aveva così la sua famiglia di Duino.

-        Dopo il doloroso scoppio della guerra dei Balcani il paese ha riempito per due volte l'intero seminterrato della scuola con abiti, prodotti alimentari e medicine, che i furgoni del collegio hanno portato a tutti i campi profughi oltre il confine sloveno e in tutti i paesi istriani dove si trovavano i campi di rifugiati.

-        Per Sutcliffe, l'apertura di ogni anno accademico doveva essere un evento anche duinese, ed era per quello che in ogni luogo in cui si svolgeva la cerimonia – Firenze, Roma, Milano, Torino, Vienna, Budapest, Strasburgo, e altri – c'erano sempre dei pullman di compaesani duinesi.

-        Per facilitare la comunicazione con la gente del villaggio, aveva stipulato che tutti i ragazzi, oltre al programma normale di studi, dovevano studiare anche la lingua italiana come materia aggiuntiva.

-        Ci sono altri esempi, in ambito individuale, nei quali il collegio sotto Sutcliffe è venuto incontro a persone in gravi difficoltà.

Per questo suo impegno nel nostro villaggio vogliamo compiere un atto in sua memoria, perché Duino è stato una parte fondamentale della sua vita. Domenica 15 dicembre, ore 11:50 – Chiesa di Duino. Vi aspettiamo.

(14)

I'm conveying a message from my father, Captain Raj Mohindra, prime mover and founding chief executive of the Mahindra UWC, which enjoyed David Sutcliffe's mentorship and support. Raj served as a midshipman under Lord Mountbatten in the Royal Navy's Mediterranean Fleet and after learning more of the UWC history upon my return from Armand Hammer UWC of the American West in 1984, resolved to fulfill

Mountbatten's dream of a UWC in India, which he accomplished after a 13 year struggle against the Indian government. I did not have the privilege of knowing David, but recall he and my father had a close relationship.

"It is with great sadness that I learnt of the demise of David Sutcliffe. I was introduced to him in 1996 by Sir Ian Gourlay, Director General, UWCs who had requested David to be the mentor of the Indian UWC project in Pune, of which I was the founding Chief Executive. When I first met him, I gained the impression that he belonged to the unique and exclusive institution of British Headmasters who have moulded generations of students not only in Great Britain but in several other parts of the world. David appeared to be a bit stern but in effect he was gentle and had a heart of gold. He was kind, sympathetic and a thorough gentleman. David played a critical role in setting up the Mahindra UWC and I am personally grateful to him as I learnt much from him. Today, all those students who came across David at the Atlantic College and those who passed through the portals of the Adriatic College when he was its Head, will remember him with great affection and admiration. He was one of the towering personalities of the UWC movement and spearheaded it with great aplomb and success during its difficult times in the formative years. I extend my condolences to Elisabeth Sutcliffe."

(15)

Caro Rettore, you were like a father to us.

Firm when it mattered but forgiving when it mattered more. Leading by example, as a principle. You have encouraged us at the right moments and lovingly corrected when we should have known better. You had deep respect for each and every member of the community and always knew how to strike the right balance between common good and good of the individual students or teachers.

You have shown us that dreams can be lived and that feet on the ground are a great help at that. You are responsible for my best educational experience as well as the best travel experience, no less (the famous Mt. Athos trip).

Rest in peace and rejoice in your legacy, for it will be alive for ages.

(16)

I thought I would share the photos below, perhaps like many of us over the last few days as we reach back into our distant memories and our old photo albums – the photos are from '86 or '87 when Mr Sutcliffe visited my home town, Perth.

You can imagine the conversation whilst my father was taking the photo – how Mr Sutcliffe was commenting on my tie, at how disappointed he was to see that it wasn't one of the classic UWC ties! Many of us will remember how, to thunderous applause he would so famously present them as gifts to all the visiting dignitaries that would pass through the college.

During that visit to Perth he spent an evening out to dinner with my family and I and then the following day we visited a few of the tourist sites (we also went to the zoo and I introduced him to a real, live kangaroo). I recall a strange feeling during his visit to Perth in that I got to spend so much time together whilst we weren't technically 'headmaster and student'.

Like most, that feeling will never completely leave me even though the truth is that I spent more time with Mr Sutcliffe during his visit to Perth than the entire time I spent in Duino (and yes, still feels odd calling him David, my parents called him David and when I called him Mr

Sutcliffe during his visit, he told me that it was ok to keep calling him 'Mr Sutcliffe'!). I got to see so much of the 'man'; mostly formal during the Duino years and then a wonderful couple of days in Perth, whilst we shared time together as a family.

A great leader that has helped shape a part of me, thank you Mrs Sutcliffe for sharing him with us, allowing him to do his work and perform his magic.

(17)

My first close encounter with Mr Sutcliffe was when sailing a laser.

I was a novice (and still am). It was a cold afternoon and the sea was rough. Suddenly, a voice said "You, follow me." For the next hour or so, I didn't know what hit me. Jump left, jump right, hold this, grab that.

I saw many lasers capsizing but not the one occupied by Mr Sutcliffe and this novice. I thought "Wow, he really knows what he is doing." He was like a maestro conducting an orchestra with every movement and note in sync. Later, I was to find out that he actually sailed solo across the Atlantic without modern navigational tools. He was a headmaster who mastered what he was doing and did not do things by half-measures.

When Mr Sutcliffe left to start UWC Adriatic during the second year, naturally he left a void. A teacher narrated that Mr Sutcliffe explained that if he (Mr Sutcliffe) listened to that naysayers that we should at least have the finance for the initial two years before we start, the new college would not have taken off. A lesson that can be learnt from this is that if an endeavour is worth embarking upon, we should not wait for everything to be perfect before we start.

I recall at one time where Mr Sutcliffe had to make an important decision to expel a student. He explained to us students as adults the reasons for this decision. He also said that he kept the letter in his drawer for three days. After three days, his conclusion was still the same, he proceeded. From Mr Sutcliffe, we learn not to make important decisions in haste or in anger.

One fine evening, I was browsing at the bookstore at the ground floor besides the multi-purpose hall. Mr Sutcliffe walked in. After a few minutes, he said to me: "Can you please hold his?" I was honoured thinking "Wow, the Headmaster ask me to hold his book." Then, he said: "Can you hold this and this too?" After quite a while, I was holding like 8-10 books and my hands were feeling tired. So, I asked a fellow student manning the bookstore "Where's DBS?" to which she replied "Oh, he left a while ago."

As many have said, Mr Sutcliffe's sense of humour was subtle. To me, it was unforgettable. And he knew more about you than you think.

A stern, visionary Headmaster with a subtle sense of humour. What a man, what a life, what a Headmaster!

(18)

I wrote a bit about DBS departure on my wall some days ago, as I always do when someone cherished starts to fly away.

Vuela alto DBS.

Everyone is sharing stories of how important and inspiring you were in their lives. I only remember the few times we exchanged words, always a fight. One could think it's a pity not to keep a nice memory of our exchanges, but ...

I still remember clearly the way you bluntly asked me: "what are YOU doing here?" When you saw me at an LSE meeting. It was my first year at university and clearly you thought it was a joke I had made it into a British university.

It was in the same cold tone you told me: "I think YOU shouldn't be here". When you caught me at 2am at Mickey's on a school day. I think you had to battle many internal contradictions in your lifetime. The fact that strong, unapologetic, young women made you uncomfortable was one of your big contradictions, and I had all the hallmarks.

I think your biggest achievement was to be bold and let 16 years old live in almost liberty without grown-ups telling us what to. It surely was a scaring thing to do and you overcome the fear, knowing it was worthy. But then again, your contradictions aroused when we didn't live up to your standards. And that was ok.

I am grateful we crossed paths, for I learnt to own being unapologetic for being strong, for being young, for being a woman ... I learnt to own the fact that I was going to get people crossed along my way, just because I was not what they expected me to be, and that it was fine. It was fine to not be liked by the Headmaster, for I was happy with myself.

Vuela alto DBS.

(19)

Dear friends, classmates, fellow middle-aged people living your lives, I was knocked quietly sideways by the news of Mr Sutcliffe's passing last week. I've always enjoyed the sense he was out there, making good in the world, even when I was not actively in touch with him. I shared my thanks and regrets about my time at UWCAD (86-88) with him through hand-written letters; he responded with sincerity, not always writing what I wanted to read/hear, but taking the time to reply thoughtfully. That quality of his, saying what needed to be said, no matter whether it was what I wished to hear, was fundamental to my respect for him. He was willing to identify the uncomfortable truth and push me to reflect on my own selfish desires rather than project those onto others.

I admired Mr Sutcliffe; I privately hoped he approved of me and my choices at the college, even afterwards. I sensed he saw through me and grasped all facets in the moment he saw me walking or lingering around Duino. He saw through all of us, grasped each situation in a moment, like he grasped the global need to grow relevant education where and when it was needed most. His attentiveness to me as a person, and others, coupled with his grasp of the global; there was room for all of us, in his mind, in his heart. This man demonstrated grace under tremendous pressures we were never privy to in our youthful bliss.

Mr Sutcliffe, you were a stellar human being. I am so very lucky to have known you and seen your live activism on the ground, face-to-face, person-to-person. What you achieved in your lifetime will stand for many of us as a colossal gift, for us, our children, their future, our future.

Thank you, my dear old teacher, mentor, headmaster, friend. I miss you. Thank you.

(20)

It's been more than a week and people keep on posting beautiful things, amazing anecdotes and I've been wondering, who was DBS for me? I do not have clear memories of him. I know that when the 1985 earthquake hit Mexico, just about 3 weeks after I first arrived in Duino he ordered Elisabetta (remember her?) to stay in his office with both me and Lizzie my second year all night or as long as it took to get news from our families. And he did not rest until we did ... Reading your posts

I remembered how he passed his hand over his hair and how he had this funny walk ... how he balanced himself on his feet when standing.

I also remembered Edward as we were close friends in Duino and I thought ... if there is a heaven I know Edward was there, with his funny smile to welcome him and I pictured a really nice father and son reunion. Both pairs of blue eyes, filled with joy. I'm now an educator myself and have come to the realization that DBS loved us all; he knew each and every one of us and would remember us long after we had left the college ... regardless of how much contact we had actually had with him and the number of posts on this site are living proof of that. The number of lives he touched is simply amazing ...

We have a saying in Mexico that says that you only die when the last person who knew you forgets you ...

So my dear DBS you are SO alive still!! So happy, happy birthday to you! Thanks again and again and again! Cheers!

(21)

In recent years, I have thought a lot of David Sutcliffe – particularly since I became a father. I have come to realize that this extraordinary universe that is parenthood brings one to view all things in a different perspective.

I used to feel that my wife and I had rather a handful with our twins, but it then dawned upon me that every year in Duino Mr Sutcliffe had over 200 kids in his charge. Young, carefree, opinionated and impetuous, and sometimes outright reckless. The mind boggles – I don't think I'd have been able to sleep at night.

I imagine that we students gave Mr and Mrs Sutcliffe a share of headaches to last them for several lifetimes. To this day, I remain in awe of their courage, resilience and resourcefulness in shouldering such an enormous commitment.

I will never forget the time he persuaded me to confess the facts of an outlandish misdemeanour to a forbidding delegation of state officials – a truly humbling experience. He stood by my side throughout the entire ordeal. When we got out, he looked me in the eye, jabbed me in the shoulder and said 'Well done, man!' I felt dizzy and weak-kneed, scorched, but – somehow – purged. Most of all, I felt grateful. Grateful for his support in that circumstance and grateful for the hard lesson he had taught me about integrity and accountability.

I will always be thankful for his exceptional fairness and foresight, for his clear example of inclusion and grace. And foremost, for being the paragon he never ceased to be, which in my adult years guided me through many of the vital choices of my life.

I am sure he was aware that many of us referred to him as 'Papà'. This was singularly appropriate, I feel, for he unfailingly stood in for our parents – discreetly, reassuringly, dependably.

For these, and many, many other reasons, I will always be in his debt.

I hope I'll be able to follow his example, and be worthy of the privilege I was granted each time I stepped across his school's threshold.

Yes, HIS school, for it is his child – and so, in many ways, are we all. With immense affection and gratitude.

(22)

Those of us who are older and weren't as lucky to have David as our headmaster and teacher, those of us who met him and helped him implement his unique projects of international education (in my case, the UWC in Mostar), we have our own stories about the reach of his vision and his firm belief that only education could save the world from wars and injustices, that international education of the kind offered by UWC is especially important because it breaks down barriers, prejudice and animosity among young people and that, as such, it should be organised in places „where it is vitally needed, and not where funds can be raised" – as David used to say.

(23)

A lot has already been said about Mr Sutcliffe and I feel proud to be among many who feel part of those memories of him.

Yet, one thing which I would like to add is a more personal touch, namely his influence on me which I can now fully appreciate being not only adult but also an active teacher. It is only recently that I have come to realise how much Mr Sutcliffe's trust in us (already mentioned here) determines the way I try to trust my students and the way I try to seek the best in them. I do strongly feel it was my experience of being in UWCAD that showed me such trust is possible (e.g. trust which allowed Mr Sutcliffe to let us freely wander around Mt Athos for five days in pre-mobile era).

I still learn than trust but I hope my students feel at least a glimpse of that sense and of the security which he gave me when I was in Duino.

(24)

One of the greatest honours (and greatest surprises) of my life was when David asked me to become his deputy in Duino (UWCAD).

Working hand-in-glove with him for four years was a privilege I am thankful for and a period in my professional life beyond compare – because of the person he was. He trusted me to get on with the job in my own way while protecting me with the shield of his huge, unassailable authority.

Working with David was exciting, unorthodox and stimulating. You never knew what would happen next, but what you could be sure of was that something would!

I well remember, when I was relatively new to the college and unused to its extraordinary pace of life, seeing a large number of students crammed in front of a notice board in the school building.

They were looking incredulously at a blue piece of paper announcing that the whole school was going to Rome the following week by special overnight train! Was this a hoax? No, it was true – and we didn't just go to Rome; we went to the Quirinale – by invitation!

UWC events like this one, soaring beyond the IB, encouraged by David, were frequent and these occasions are probably what most students and staff remember best. There were, of course, routines, but they were never dull and the here-and-now was always part of the bigger picture, consciously framed within and driven by the College's mission. David was inseparable from this mission and his charisma kept it alive and in the forefront of our minds.

I can now imagine him getting impatient and saying, "This is all very well, but what are you going to DO now?" The last time Henry and I saw David was twelve days before he died. It was an effort for him to speak but he wanted to talk about two subjects: the paintings of Piero della Francesca and the future of UWC.

He never alluded to his illness except in so far as it had denied him the vigor to pursue his life's work – the furthering of the essential spirit of UWC education in places where it is needed as the movement grows.

On thinking about this precious last meeting, it seems to me that his moral courage and power to act arose not only from personal charisma and his determination to do what he believed was right and necessary, but also from the fact that he wasn't held back by worries of what people thought of him, or by personal vanity. So, „What are we going to do now?" It is up to us to do our best to carry on his work and „take a leaf out of his book".

Those hundreds, probably thousands, of us who were lucky enough to have been touched by his life, and feel indebted to him, can make a difference. If we all do something material in support of his vision, we too can become a formidable force – and if we do, I think he would be proud – or at least satisfied.

(25)

I did not know Mr Sutcliffe well. Like many others, I had a certain respect for him which meant there was a largely impenetrable distance between us.

He was the older British headmaster, I was yet another messy and confused teenager happy to be a million miles from home but not fully capable of managing my life, studies and emotions in the magical and at time absurd bubble of UWC Adriatic. His job was not to be my friend, his job was to create the conditions in which I and my peers could thrive as humans. And what a job he did at that.

In my first year at the Adriatic in the late 90th I found myself more than once in need of support. I also found myself having quite a few 'difficult' conversations with Mr Sutcliffe. He would do his trademark face rub and he would not say many more words than strictly necessary.

But I had no doubt, no doubt whatsoever, that he had my best interest and welfare at heart. When I needed it the most, Mr Sutcliffe asked me if I was alright. It might have seemed like a small gesture, but at that time it was exactly the kind of concern and compassion that with razor sharp precision helped me to navigate some rather difficult times.

Together with the then Director of Studies Sandy Thomas he took an active interest in making sure I didn't suffer homophobic abuse and also asked how this aspect of College life was going. The most awkward conversation we ever had was probably when he (after some intense face rubbing) felt he needed to remind me of the 'no intimacy' rule at the school and that it applied to everyone regardless of sexuality.

It makes for a good anecdote and while awkward at the time, today I look back with a smile at how he was capable of stepping out of his comfort zone to ensure both student welfare and that the integrity of College rules were followed (or at least that we felt compelled to pretend we followed them).

In my second year, I was in a much better place than I was in my first year and the conversations with Mr Sutcliffe were fewer. He did stop me a few times on my way from my daily runs on the Rilke path to make sure I was eating properly (for reference, I was, the running just made me lose weight).

The year after I graduated I came back to the College to visit my first years (by then in their second year).

One day I went for a run on Rilke path for old times' sake. As I came back I met Mr Sutcliffe on Fore lawn. 'Still running are you?' he asked. 'And how are things in London?' I had no idea he knew that I by then studied in London, I hadn't told him, we weren't close like that.

I realised that he must have in one way or another kept track of where all the ex-students ended up. I think in that sense that while he was not teaching classes at Adriatic, we were all his pupils and he took an active interest in all of us, whether we knew it or not.

And as we were all his pupils, he was our teacher. The experience he created for all of us at Adriatic taught me, and continues to teach me, a lot.

Thank you, Mr Sutcliffe.

(26)

I first found out that Mr Sutcliffe passed away from Bogna J. Glassen-Obidzinska.

It was the first thing I read as soon as I woke up and I felt a sense of loss all day ... the more posts I read about David, the more I realised why his loss has left such an impact on all of us. Being an educator I can now appreciate much more what an amazing leader he was ... in his own way. Possibly the most striking attributes were that he truly believed in the values of UWC and that he appreciated the hard work of the teachers ... and as a teacher I know that that makes a huge difference to the sense of community. No wonder that after so many years I still feel close to all my friends (including teachers) from Duino.

Thank you David ... and thank you Elisabeth for always supporting such an amazing man.

(27)

Having been at AC from 77-79, I did not have that many contact with DBS, but unconsciously I always felt that he as a headmaster made sure, that AC would go on, despite the financial worries at that time.

Working in education today, more precisely at University in sustainable development, I can only see with the years how much David had done for us – despite a certain distance he always kept, you could feel how important every single student was for him.

It was only with the years, that I realised how much I appreciated David Sutcliffe and today I can valuate how important values are in your life – they give you guidance.

Thank you so much David!

(28)

Having compulsively read every single contribution to this group since the beginning, I am pained by how much I didn't know about Mr Sutcliffe.

At the end of the first term of my first year in Duino, I booked a flight back home to Hong Kong that was a couple of days before term officially finished. (Why? I can't remember ... but if I have to guess it would have something to do with unavailable flights for a long journey that I didn't have a lot of experience dealing with as a 16-year-old who never spent any time abroad!!!) I remember breaking the news to Mr Sutcliffe in the school building, maybe in the staff room or just outside. There was silence for what felt like an eternity, and eventually he walked off.

Knowing myself, I would have been quietly panicking about that for days, first for having to commit the travesty itself, and secondly for having to tell DBS, with whom I hadn't exchanged a word until then.

Perhaps I expected some understanding at best or at worst a stern telling off ... but the "froideur" I experienced really left a mark on my non-existent relationship with Mr Sutcliffe. I stayed well clear of him from then on. Maybe deep down I didn't feel that I was worthy of his attention, just like I didn't expect the headmistress at my old covent school would know who I was. To me they were distant adults and figures of authority who might as well live in a different universe. And on top of that I really committed the worst crime by deciding to hightail out of college 2 days before I was allowed to!

Now that I am middle-aged and understand how much will power and effort David must have exerted so that all the stars aligned and this blank-slate-of-a-girl found herself tumbling in and out of the whirlwind that was 2 precious formative teenage years in that remote corner in Italy ...

I would not be who I am now without you, David, and no, I am not an investment banker. For that, and for everything else that you have given to all the young adults that pass through a UWC, thank you.

You are in my thoughts, Elisabeth!

(29)

Dear Elisabeth,

I have been thinking of David and you and your family over the last sad weeks, and so many memories have come up. My first memory of David from my first year at AC in 1972 is that of an awe–inspiring stern British headmaster, who expected us all to perform at our very best, and to go beyond what we thought we were able to do, as he also showed he was doing himself, both in his adventures at sea and in his dedication to expand the UWC network, to build new schools in places that others may not have chosen because they were in difficult environments.

I have fond memories of the few times we sailed together, mixed memories of our conversation when he asked me to speak on behalf of the students at the Arthur Rubenstein fundraising concert in London, I told him I was scared and could not do it, he told me I could and should and would, so I did, and survived! I have often thought of that moment later in life when having to do things that were not so easy, and I am eternally grateful for that ' you can do it' trust he had in us students, a very profound trust and belief in young people which I have met in only few educators. It was always difficult for me, even many years later, when David came to support us in the German Committee, and when we met in other places, to actually not call him 'Mr Sutcliffe' , but David.

Sincerely, A.

(30)

It struck me how tolerant DBS was.

I ran into "Him" so many times on the Piazza after midnight and he never said a thing. Well, I always had 5-6 books with me at all times, held them close to my chest and looked either too tired or too harmless of a nerd; he probably didn't think I was worthy of a stern look.

I liked his speeches, even the stern ones. He was a very good orator. I didn't always like what he said, his passion for outdoors is still so not my thing but I couldn't fail respecting how he managed to keep on top of everything at all times (or creating the illusion thereof). Great wizard, a little bit of Dumbledore, a little bit of Snape, but more of an idealist than either of those fiction characters.

I apparently managed to piss him off for leaving the college right after the IB exams, without telling him. I had my reasons. He sent my father one angry telex and then it was all history of course. Although I remained a bit bitter about it, again never could fail to respect him for managing to "scare me" from miles away.

Truth is I didn't want to say goodbye to anybody. I still am horrible at that. But this time, I so want to do the right thing. So thank you and goodbye for one last time, Mr Sutcliffe. This world is a better place because of you and I hope I can give back a fraction of what you inspired.

(31)

I have very fond memories of David in Duino, from encouraging us with the editing of the Noema manifesto, to energetically supporting the Walkathon to Trieste, and rescuing my housemates from the Yugoslav police when they inadvertently crossed the border. I just found, in an old box, the card that he and Elisabeth sent to thank me for writing to them when their son Edward sadly passed away in 1993.

David wrote a few words on the card with his trademark spider handwriting. He also kindly wrote to me a couple of years later to congratulate me for getting my undergraduate degree in the UK (I never worked out how he found out about it!). Berta and I then saw David and Elisabeth again in London a few years later – it must have been roughly 15 years ago – and had a very nice afternoon in their house in Pimlico. Unfortunately, I never saw him again after that.

I am very grateful for all he did for us former, current and future UWC-ers.

(32)

I met Mr Sutcliffe in 1984. I took sailing with him. I remember, in my poor English, understanding that once he sailed from England all the way to Italy. I believe that he said that he held the rope with his teeth during a sea storm and injured some of the front teeth as the rope snapped. Maybe I misunderstood him. I always admired him and he was my father figure while at the UWC. A friend of mine from Zimbabwe came for a weekend with me to visit my home in Rijeka, then Yugoslavia. She couldn't reenter Italy and we got stuck at the border. She and I panicked. He appeared in a flash and made the impossible possible and she returned to Duino in no time.

He was a great father to his beloved son Edward! I remember Mr Sutcliffe interacting with some of the Italian parents when Edward, others students and I came back from the two weeks scuba diving trip from Malta. Mrs Sutcliffe has always been wonderful to me and she is in my thoughts and prayers during this difficult time of loss.

(33)

A precious gift from David

I have been reading the comments posted here with a deeply felt sentiments of nostalgia of times under David's headship.

The feeling of worth in the things we did everyday was always present, even in the most ordinary things of daily life. That sentiment of nostalgia and the pride in achieving together the ideals of the college was something that David helped to instil in subtle ways and explicitly sometimes. He fostered whatever humble virtue we might have had and drove it into its greatest potential level of achievement.

There are many examples of ways in which my life as a teacher was driven to levels of accomplishment of which I was not aware. One dramatic event comes to my mind instantaneously: the moment when one of our students – a member of my tutorial group – suddenly fell into an ailment condition that put him at a critical risk of losing his life.

It was on one of the first days of April, 1998 when the boy came to our Pala house and told me of a pain he had on his leg, despite the fact that he had suffered a minor bruise low on his left foot resulting from his last session of his basketball activity.

My first reaction was to inform our college doctor and she promptly came to the college to visit the boy. The doctor then called me to say that there was something suspicious in his pain and she dreaded the possibility that it might be a life threatening case of septic shock and she was swiftly calling an ambulance to take the boy to the local Monfalcone Hospital where, on confirmation of the feared initial suspicion, he was taken to the intensive care unit. I must mention that some minutes before our lady doctor had come to Duino to check, the boy was visited by Fernando Piccinini, an Argentinean ex student who himself was a doctor and he briefly visited my tutee and told us with a concerned face: "it is a septic shock". Immediately after having taken the boy to hospital, together with Dr Possarelli we went to David's office to brief him about this so sad and critical event. There and then I saw David expressing his concern and immediately taking action. His first move was to inform the parents and ask for them, or one of them, to travel to Duino as early as possible. Then he requested the doctor to keep him briefed at all moments.

Afterward he himself went to hospital to talk to the medical staff. I observed great pain and concern in his face but not a moment of hesitation about his course of action in front of a crisis. As I left David's office, I found Fernando again and told him that at Monfalcone Hospital they were making arrangements to transfer the boy to another city, I think it was Padova, where there was a specialised unit. Fernando then observed that time was crucial in these cases and maybe it was better for the boy to be treated immediately at Monfalcone. I mentioned this to our doctor. She said that she also thought the same and phoned the hospital and, after some pondering by the head doctor, the request was agreed upon. Immediate arrangements were made for the new course of action.

I also telephoned the parents to assure them that I would take care for them in case they were coming to Duino. As I learned that the mother had just made arrangements to take the first combination of flights available to come to Duino, I took note of the arrival and assured the lady that I would pick her up at the airport, pay a brief visit to hospital to see how the boy was doing and then come to Pensione Aurora where I had booked a room for her.

I cannot emphasize enough the courage of that boy to stand the surgical operation that the doctors followed in order to trace the course of the infection on his leg and attack it directly there with appropriate antibiotics.

Then I felt that a spontaneous rapport of affection developed with the boy's mum. I remember her eyes so vividly, her profound serenity and the moving love expressed when we went to the boy's room and found the most phenomenal untidiness you can imagine. There was a touching tenderness in the way she started folding some garment, putting into boxes the vast variety of tinned and packed cooking ingredients mixed with everything else. Love can be expressed in the folding of a tee-shirt, I thought.

As I had to carry on with my teaching, everyday before 7 o'clock in the morning I took the mum to hospital where we both were allowed to see the boy before the daily medical check. One happy day the doctors informed us that the infection had been completely removed.

One aspect of this event calls for important consideration: the solidarity and support colleagues gave to the boy. He had asked me to bring all his college textbooks and notes and, as much as it was permitted, he attempted to reconstruct his usual mess piling his books in every surface available around his bed. Henry will remember the extent to which the boy went into memorizing one of Shakespeare's dramas.

When the boy left the college, he had to undergo his military service and was found perfectly fit for that obligation and had to spend at least a year, I presume, submerged in mud and surrounded with mosquitoes in the jungle, as he wrote to me. Accomplished that, he then could take up his place at Cambridge University, then another degree at Harvard moving afterward to a very successful professional career as Investment Manager of his government, then Vice-President of Ortus Capital Management Ltd. and currently as partner in Call Levels Corp.

On the following day the boy was released from hospital, when his mum was making arrangements to go back home, I found a huge bouquet of flowers in our Staff Common Room with the greatest treasure I have received from my absent headmaster. It was this blue note that was typed so as to facilitate understanding.

I thank David for that acknowledgment and for the outstanding way in which he exercised his function as a Headmaster, better put, as The Headmaster.

Thank you, David.

(34)

Farewell, old sailor. No further fee shall be levied, the ferryman honoured to have you on board.

(35)

Five years after College ended and one year after I got my Fine Arts Diploma I left for India alone, planning to spend there almost a year. I flew to Kolkata in October 1993 and in May 1994 I was around Mumbai, quite tanned by the time, had lost some weight and was getting used to being a Gipsy. Traveling by train all the time was wonderful. Life had a big heart for me and I felt a big heart for life: everything was possible and nothing was dangerous. I was far from everything known.

One day I took the ferry from Mumbai to Elephanta Island to visit the famous caves. The sun was shining and the wind blew softly. I was inside the cave and stopped to contemplate a carved pillar when somebody stumbled from behind the pillar and almost fell in front of me. I slightly jerked and looked at the stumbler: it was Mr Sutcliffe. I was silenced by shock: was that real?? He was amused by my face and smiled. His hand automatically touched his hair. I couldn't recover from the shock. He smiled at me and said something casual, then he pulled me out of the cave to share the surprise with Elisabeth.

You should have seen her face when she saw us walking out together! We took the ferry back to Mumbai and they invited me to lunch. Elisabeth wanted ice cream for dessert but the other lady insisted she should try lychees. She said ok, I'll have lychees provided they come with ice cream. The lady said yes, of course, but when desserts came Elisabeth only got a bowl of lychees and no ice cream at all. Everybody was engaged in the conversation and nobody noticed it but me. She looked at me and smiled and didn't say a word. Her eyes shone with irony and disenchantment – they said to me: well, you can't always get what you want. I wonder why memory preserves such details for years and years – 25 to be precise – and leaves me with no clue of what we talked about at lunch instead.

Now I realize in those six years between 1988 and 1994 they had met some 800 new students in Duino ... but in the dark cave he recognised me before I recognised him. They were so warm, it was like feeling in family again. When they went back to Italy Elisabeth called my parents to tell them I was in good health and safe.

(36)

The first time I met him we were at the Italian selections in 1988. During the interview I boasted that, should they accept me, I would start a student newspaper at the college.

Sutcliffe looked at me in the eye and asked me, in his excellent Italian, which newspaper I'd suggest a foreigner to read in order to get an idea of what Italian society was like.

I mentioned a few, carefully selecting those newspapers that included different political points of view: left, right, center.

Sutcliffe's face was like a stone sculpture. He did not seem impressed. I felt I had to come up with something smarter, so I quickly added that, in order to *really* understand Italy, one must read *La Gazzetta dello Sport*.

No smile. Nothing. He just scribbled something on a piece of paper and said the interview was over. I told myself I had just blown my chances. Thankfully, I was wrong.

The last time I met him we were at the 2010 reunion in Duino. I told him that I had an 11-year-old daughter, and I hoped one day she could have the same life-shaping experience I had had at the college.

He sincerely wished me good luck and we shook hands with big smiles. I remember thinking that age had made him softer. The wine at the lunch table too, maybe.

Now that he is gone and so many people are sharing their memories of him, I marvel at how tremendously coherent his life was. I think a lot about that, and I think about my schoolmates from 1988-90, about the kids I selected in Rome some years ago, about the ones who will be going to the colleges in the future, and I take some comfort imagining the connection, the bond that ties us all together through time. Yet, above all, I have this rather strange feeling: I miss him. Even though I had no contacts with him in so many years, I feel as if I lost someone very dear to me. I don't know why.

Maybe age has made me soft too. And the wine as well, of course.

(37)

I must confess that I had an intense and somehow turbulent relationship with DBS. In part, that was because my father was also the Principal of Colégio Santa Cruz, a Canadian school founded by two priests, Father Lionel Corbeil and Father Paul Eugéne Charbonneau, a kind of local Kurt Hahn. It was due to his tenacity and inventiveness that Santa became the best school in São Paulo and the first one to send students to UWCs. He made Santa Cruz a place that was the sole educational stronghold against Brazilian dictatorship, which lasted for 21 long years from 1964 to 1985. At Santa, Father Charbonneau showed movies that were forbidden by governmental censorship agency, such as Christiane F. – Wir Kinder vom Bahnhof Zoo, shocking Brasilian church too.

He was always at TV shows and used to wear red when defending conservative ideas and clergymen when defending very revolutionary theses, as women liberation, sexuality, or marijuana consumption – he was favor to legalization already in the sixties. Also, he was seen drinking with students, beer or whiskey, and in company of beautiful women late at night.

My father succeed Corbeil as a Headmaster. Also, my uncle, his brother, was the dean at one of the best federal universities in Brazil. My father met David in Duino. He had a meeting with him to discuss if I had to do leave school because of my hearing loss and awful academic performance at the beginning of my first year, something that I think would be unbelievable nowadays ...

But, I am especially grateful to Mr Sutcliffe and also to Elizabeth. Both were my tutors. They took me by the hands and made me understand and learn that nothing in life is easy; for everything that you earn, you have to work hard, and sometimes you have to do painfully.

DBS knew that Maria Teresa, the Italian teacher who died of cancer during our first year, liked me very much and cared about my future. She was especially concerned about the bad habits I had – heavy drinking and smoking – much like an average Latin American boy, always running after any nice skirt.

One day David came up to me and said: let's visit Maria Teresa in the hospital, it's going to be a farewell. He knew she was dying and he was right, it happened days after we went there, and I remember all the words she said to me: "Luiz, you are intelligent, pretty and funny, everybody likes you, but you have to take care. "Smoke less, drink less and sleep more," She was right. I quitted cigarettes, still, smoke cigars in particular situations, but couldn't handle sleeping more. So, for me, David was half a father, half the incredible headmaster he was, in fact.

In the second year's yearbook, I wrote something and quoted the final of the lyric of The Boxer, a song I loved and still love, by Paul Simon and Art Garfunkel. So, to finish, excuse me for such long text. Let me quote the lyric again, pointing out that now the years are rolling by me; they are rocking easily. I am older than I once was and younger than I'll be. But, that's not unusual, no, it isn't strange; changes after changes, we are more or less the same. Thanks, DBS and Elizabeth, to allow me to be part of your lives, you were very important for me.

The Boxer

(...)
Now the years are rolling by me
They are rocking easily
I am older than I once was
And younger than I'll be
But that's not unusual
No, it isn't strange
After changes upon changes
We are more or less the same
After changes we are
More or less the same
Then I'm laying out my winter clothes
And wishing I was gone
Going home
Where the New York City winters
Aren't bleeding me
Leading me
Going home
In the clearing stands a boxer
And a fighter by his trade
And he carries the reminders
Of ev'ry glove that laid him down
Or cut him till he cried out
In his anger and his shame
"I am leaving; I am leaving."
But the fighter still remains...

(38)

I entered the college in 1990 with the enthusiasm, idealism and expectations of a 16 year old who had spent the last few years in a school where academic performance and unconditional respect of rules and authority where the meter against which I felt I was judged on daily basis. UWC has been a life changing experience and with my broken English (learning foreign languages at that time was not considered a priority for Italian pupils) I had very little sense of what was expecting me. When in the first days of school I was told I had to "choose" my IB subject I was not sure I understood it well. Really??? Did I get to choose what I prefer to study?

Life was looking really good and my first months in Duino will remain in my heart as a time of special encounters and life lasting memories, and I know some of you out there can recognize why and share this feeling. In spite of my English improving speedily, thanks to some special help from special people, and my school performance attaining acceptable results, I was not quite yet into participating in public events or daring public speaking. The legacy of my rigid Italian school imposed some sort of barrier to me and I continued to function better in small groups. Mr Sutcliffe really had a special eye for understanding young people. I never really had much interaction with him as he did inspire in me great respect and some sort of intimidation.

When the first semester reports came home most teachers sent positive remarks. At the end of them came his hand written final comment which I will never forget. It said something like: "Maria had a very good start of the year. I have been observing her and hers is the type of voice one would like to hear more in students assemblies and events. I encourage her to make herself heard more in public!" You would not imagine, Mr Sutcliffe how many times I repeated those words to myself later in life when I was indeed facing large audiences with the same sense of discomfort I use to have at 16.

Thank you for helping us understand that our voices are worth hearing and that we have a responsibility to use it for the best.

(39)

When I arrived to Atlantic College in 1979, one of the things that baffled me was that we called teachers by their first names. Bob, Paul, Jane, Bill, Catherine, James, Jesús ... But Mr Sutcliffe was Mr Sutcliffe, or DBS among us students, so it's quite surprising to me that many posters here refer to him as David. Perhaps things changed with time.

At AC, Mr Sutcliffe seemed stern, distant, concentrated and efficient. Most certainly not a headmaster I'd call by his first name. Other than pulling him up from the audience to teach him a dance during a national evening, there were only a few occasions when I spoke to him. So I didn't think I'd ever cross paths with him after leaving AC. How wrong I was.

We first met again in Duino, when UWC alumni from what was then Yugoslavia met for a reunion in Ljubljana in 1988 and took a trip to Adriatic College. Soon afterwards Yugoslavia disintegrated, new countries emerged, and war ensued. Under Mr Sutcliffe's leadership, UWC Adriatic made sure to accept students from all ex-YU countries throughout the 1990th, creating an opportunity for students from the conflicted countries to live together, forge friendships and foster understanding. It was not always easy, but it was possible.

He encouraged Adriatic College students to work with the refugees, to be aware of what was going on in the "neighbourhood". It was then that the Croatian alumni became involved with the selections, and subsequently founded the National Committee, which I was honoured to chair. There was so much to learn, so much to handle. Mr Sutcliffe was always on the other side of the letter, fax, or phone, always ready to help. He offered advice when my colleagues and I needed it, he wrote letters, came for meetings, tried to open doors to potential supporters when we began to fundraise, had our back when some people attempted to meddle with fair selections, supported our participation in international meetings, and included us in his endeavour to found an UWC in Mostar and have students from Croatia at the college from the onset.

He asked for details about how best to work in Croatia because each country is different. In all the years of our post-AC communication Mr Sutcliffe was kind, understanding, and reliable.

My husband met him and came to admire him (they always spoke German). He may have retired as HM or rettore but he never retired from UWC. He envisioned projects that have yet to be developed, like a multiethnic school in Vukovar, because he thought "It must become our joint task to take international education not to where it can be afforded, but to where it is really and urgently needed."

I can't possibly express my gratitude to Mr Sutcliffe for first trusting me with a scholarship, then for his unwavering support to our NC, and for his tireless work for the UWC, especially for the students and communities in our corner of the world. Also, I have just checked. He signed all his emails to me with "David".

(40)

DAVID SUTCLIFFE

I was fortunate to work at AC 1973-77 during a time of growth. My first Impression on approaching St. Donat's Castle was of a "throwback" into British Public School ethos and values. This was quickly dispelled as I learned more (pre-internet!).

Meeting with David for the first time, I was struck by his aura of distinction, purpose and ease, and of a fundamental kindness. During my time as Music Instructor at AC, this never changed. I learned that he trusted his staff, listened as well as making decisions, offered opportunity for growth, new ideas. And amidst his extraordinary list of accomplishments and responsibilities, which no public award could sufficiently honor, he never lost sight of and concern for each person's individuality.

As a professional novice at that time, I also felt I was on a "scholarship" at AC, that it was a special privilege to work under his leadership, and that he was approachable for any problem to solve or advise on. Despite not being central to the UWC mission, music was never sidelined. He and Elisabeth cared about every aspect of life. After several intervening decades, we reconnected, and I felt very touched by a deep sense of friendship with this remarkable family.

How many students and colleagues have felt and still feel this! So many of our lives are indebted, inwardly and outwardly, to our connection with UWCs and David's personal contributions.

His vision, his books, his leadership and his friendship leave a legacy that I cherish and will never forget.

(41)

UWC selections at L'Aquila, Italy 1988. I was having my interview with the committee and DBS was there. He asked me something about my motivational letter ... honestly I told him that my mum wrote it and he really appreciated it.

Well many years after he was still remembering it and kidding me about it that was DBS ...

(42)

Dear Mr Sutcliffe,

during my stay at the college in Duino (1988-1990) you were such an authority for me that I never really found the courage to talk to you. Due to my huge respect, I was simply too shy in your presence.

But one thing I am grateful for is your tolerance that you showed, after Megan (Zanatta) and I had been arrested by actually very nice Italian police on the highway next to Vicenza, while trying to hitchhike back to Duino at about 21:00 in the dark. After a short trip to Verona Megan and I were supposed to go on our project week to Paris a few days after that.

Unfortunately the police in Vicenza contacted the college as Megan and I were hoping that they would give us a ride straight to Duino all the way from Vicenza (nice plan ...), because we didn't want to spend our money on the train tickets! – So we simply told the police that we had no money left and therefore couldn't afford the train back to Duino! (To our excuse, please consider that we made this plan at the age of 16/17, and at that time I was convinced that everything was possible and nothing could stop us !!!)

Well, the policemen then called Manuel Fernandez, who was on duty in Duino that evening, and told him that he had to come to Vicenza to pick us up personally and take us back to Duino ... That was a shock for us, so, fortunately, all of a sudden, just the right amount of money happened to be found (by me) in my pocket and therefore the police kindly took us to the train station and we returned back by train, full of bad conscience and of fear, imagining the consequences that would expect us back in the college.

We arrived in Monfalcone quite late at night ...

Maybe around midnight ...

As I said before, that day Manuel Fernandez was on duty and therefore was already waiting for us and then took us back to Duino. Luckily he was smiling as always and was friendly and kind, as if nothing bad had happened (Dear Manuel! Thank you so much for that kindness! Meg and I were so grateful for that!)

We were fearing the worst ...

We were so afraid that, because of this incident, Mr Sutcliffe would AT LEAST decide to cancel our project week in Paris to punish us for what we had done (as we all know, hitchhiking was strictly forbidden at the college).

Maybe we were a bit lucky, too, because that day Mr Sutcliffe was not in Duino as he had already started his project week sailing with a group of students somewhere far away ...

So, Meg and I ended up going to Paris and having the time of our life (apart from doing research on the bicentennial of the French revolution – of course !)

After the project week we knew that there was still something to come. Luckily my tutor was Mark Silvester, who just told me with his smile, which we all know, that we did a bit of a stupid thing, but he made me understand that for him it was not really a big deal, and we just shouldn't do such a stronzata again e basta. (So, dear Mark, thanks also to you for your coolness and your understanding for the spirit of two crazy teenage girls on their way to explore the world!!!)

Mr Sutcliffe never said a word to me about what had happened.

I was just informed that he would write a letter to Megan's and my parents. I warned my father that a letter would come.

Mr Sutcliffe's letter turned out to be just a short information about our adventure. It didn't contain more than that. No disciplinary measures, no punishment. I was very relieved and grateful!

Maybe he acted like that due to the fact that Megan and I had never done anything forbidden until then and always behaved well ...

But looking at the pic, which I found in the yearbook 1989/90, I believe that inspite of his function and his responsibility as our headmaster he also had this young spirit inside his heart with a deep understanding for adolescent, enthusiastic, euphoric but sometimes still a bit silly teenagers like we used to be!

(43)

"He sought the best in people and encouraged them to embrace their passion, their skill, their talent, their vision ("You have more in you than you know" he said, quoting Hahn), but always gave that celebration of individualism a clear context: it was to serve a greater good." Read a moving tribute by Thomas Henry, former UWC Adriatic teacher, to his friend and former colleague, David B. Sutcliffe – former Head of UWC Atlantic College the founding Head of UWC Adriatic and co-founder of UWC Mostar.

Tribute by Henry Thomas, former colleague of David at UWC Adriatic and friend.

Where to begin?

David Sutcliffe was a very remarkable man: a visionary and a leader; a charismatic figure without vanity; always a teacher and always wishing to learn (his interests were myriad); a man of action (who sailed single-handed across the Atlantic in 1976); and a man of deep reflection, especially about the role of education in a fractured, dangerous, "globalised" world.

He was also the man who played the "village idiot" in a staff production of the Victorian melodrama "Maria Martin or the Red Barn", rehearsed in secret and performed for the students in the courtyard of Duino Castle. He was the van driver who carried a group of students across the Balkans to Mount Athos where they spent Project Week walking from monastery to monastery, listening and talking with those they met. He (and Elisabeth) made it a priority to attend all student shows, plays and musical performances (he was a driving force behind the creation of the Scuola di Musica) and the Sunday evening, student-led International Affairs sessions. He attached a particular importance to these because he thought them vital to a UWC education.

When the College made a "public appearance" in Friuli-Venezia Giulia or in Rome, David was always present, walking with and speaking for the college community. For David, I think, the College was more than a school. It was a community dedicated to a wider purpose: the academic, extra-curricular, pastoral, social and communal life were all directed to the aims now captured in the mission statement. What struck me and enthused me when I first came to Duino was that David argued (sometimes against stubborn resistance) that there could be no hierarchical distinction between the academic, the extra-curricular and the pastoral life of the college: they were different but all essential to the community's purpose. It was this dedication to a common purpose – shared by all staff and students, living together – that created the ethos, the "atmosphere" and experience of UWC life.

In part, this "idealist" view of collegiate life was shaped, as he often and forcefully told me, by his experience during the war years at an English boarding school on the Yorkshire moors. There he'd been given his love of languages by teachers with a passion for their subjects, and discovered the rigorous pleasures of the outdoor life, running on the Fells. I vividly recall the fascinated incredulity of a group of students in the Mensa when David recounted one school experience, prompted by a casual remark that the heating yet again was not working in Foresteria. He told us that in his time at school, pupils were required to sleep with their windows open two inches even during winter and would often find a sprinkling of snow on their blankets in the morning! His presence at lunch-time in the Mensa, eating together with students and staff, was fundamental to how he conceived his role as Rettore.

He was, of course, "The Responsible", the authority who exercised the final say, but he was also a man who invited and heeded the counsel of his students and staff. Every day there were conversations formal and informal; there were weekly Monday 7.40 am meetings with teachers, and regular full college meetings. Very often he was available in his office well into the evening and when crises occurred, (as they did!), he invited anyone to come and speak to him in confidence ("before midnight"). David took seriously the views of other people even when he profoundly disagreed with them.

He sought the best in people and encouraged them to embrace their passion, their skill, their talent, their vision ("You have more in you than you know" he said, quoting Hahn), but always gave that celebration of individualism a clear context: it was to serve a greater good. That sense of purpose was, I believe, the product of a very specific set of experiences: his experience of being a five year old evacuee in Lincolnshire from German-occupied Guernsey (where his doctor father remained for the duration of the war); his experience of reading German and French at Cambridge in the immediate post-war years; and crucially his years at Salem where he met Kurt Hahn. But the man was more than the sum of his "experiences and influences"; he possessed a generosity of spirit, an imaginative sympathy, an acute intelligence and a kindness which made him loved, as many tributes on his passing testify.

I am paying tribute to David, I am also paying tribute to Elisabeth. Of her, David wrote the following:

„Nothing would have been possible without Elisabeth….Where would I have been and how would I have managed without her?"

(44)

I remember once, when a group of students had had the hilarious idea of throwing all the benches in the dining hall out the window. At assembly that morning, DBS was furious and gave us a right talking to because there was nowhere for the kitchen staff to sit to eat their breakfast before serving ours. He had the whole lot of us file to the dining room and put the benches back before we were allowed to do anything else. It was a good lesson to show us that no member of the AC community was more important than any other.

Another time, because of the vagaries of the tides, we'd launched X23 late to sail to Pembroke. I was the navigator and had set a direct course, but the weather turned nasty and DBS asked me to plot another course, keeping close to land. It was actually a rather dangerous situation, but he never checked my course. I appreciated the confidence.

May he rest in peace. My thoughts are with his family.

(45)

Mr Sutcliffe was quite the formidable man. I respected him, but there was also a dose of (healthy?) fear. I had never heard such a posh accent in real life before! I never had a particularly close relationship with him, but I always respected him, and felt he had our backs, though on one occasion I remember that I didn't respect one of his decisions.

I got all fired up, and together with Birte we went to his office to tell him our Walkathon woes. I remember that at one point I had become so worked up that my fist was clenched, and I accidentally let it fall down on his marble table. (As soon as I had let it happen, I think I sucked in whatever oxygen was left in the room expecting my imminent expulsion). He just sat there, did his trademark face rub, followed by his signature smirk, and said, "I can see you care passionately about this!" (GULP!)

This morning Eric posted a photo that I have never owned or seen, but the image has lived with me (haunted me) all of my life – The day Mr Sutcliffe asked me to accompany Prime Minister Prodi around the campus.

"Whatever you do," said Sutcliffe, "do NOT ask if Mr Prodi has been here before! He was fundamental in the early stages of setting this UWC up. And whatever you do, do not let those bossy bodyguards push you away from him, because they will try, and once you're on the wrong side of them, you won't be able to get back in".

The entire time we were walking around the village my inner voice was busy repeating to myself:

"Don't ask him if he has been here before! Don't ask him if he has been here before!"

At which point, and this photo captures the exact second perfectly, I asked, very nervously:

"So, is it your first time here?"

The glare I got from Mr Sutcliffe cut through me like a knife. I quickly followed it up with "... on the Rilke Path?"

And the smile that followed made it all right. (I had never met a Prime Minister before – or since – and the security guards WERE intense!). I also remember him referring it to it a few days later with a sarcastic smile, which of course I deserved.

I always thought about how tight Mr and Mrs Sutcliffe were as a couple and as a team. Always together. Creating a family together, losing a son together, creating colleges together, making memories together, and impacting lives together.

Elisabeth, my thoughts are with you and your children. I cannot imagine what it must be like to have lost your "media naranja".

I am now a Headmaster and often find myself, in times when I need to pretend that I am annoyed or frustrated by a student's behaviour, buying some time and creating some atmosphere by taking my glasses off and imitating one of Sutcliffe's legendary face rubs. They help me focus, allow me to think what he might have done or said, and bring a little smirk to my face.

Mr Sutcliffe, may you rest in peace, and live long in the hearts and minds of your Duinesi, your "splendidi", and absolutely everyone who passes through UWCAD and UWCiM.

(46)

1975 Mr Sutcliffe was very much the senior man on the campus and I had little personal communication with him however I am trying hard to remember the day the canons on the front law were turned to wards the castle aiming at his office!

The canons were very heavy and it was not easy to do. It created quite a huge furore and David was more angry than I had ever known him. I think it was a protest when a student had been expelled. I wish I could remember more but it was hush hush as to who had been involved, perhaps Philippe might know ?

David Sutcliffe was very much held in awe by us students at the time but so quickly he offered real friendship when we became adults and visited the college and UWC events. A man committed to the cause who accomplished so much for so many.

(47)

Great Headmaster when I was a AC student, remembered as a typical Englishman, for his politeness and sense of humour, and a great UWCer.

(48)

Many of you already wrote much. David was one important person of our lives.

That's a fact.

One night at 1 am in a week day – I was sneaking out from a residence not mine – I met him in Duino just around the corner. After an initial exchange "you are not supposed to be around at this time" he invited me at home and we had a night long, scotch based conversation.

That's when I understood he was not only a great headmaster, he was a great man.

(49)

I will not forget David B. Sutcliffe as long as I'm alive. I don't think I was his favorite student or model teenager, and I used to avoid his path. I was the weird boy from Jordan who didn't seem to get anything right.

Yet, once he saved my life!

I was hopelessly training on canoeing (kayaking), and when the torturing session was finally over, I couldn't get myself out of my canoe, perhaps due to my oversized body. So he called out to me with his stern voice: "don't be silly ... capsize and pull yourself out." You can guess what came next; I capsized but failed to pull myself out and in a split second I was fighting for dear life.

In another second or two that felt like eternity, he swam over to me and with his strong arm muscles turned me over like you would do to a poor tortoise that had toppled over.

(50)

I still remember vividly the speech he gave at our graduation in June 1994. He said that it did not matter what we would become as long as we pursued our passions and strove to be the best at what we did.

He told us how one of his students had become a baker and now baked the best bread he had ever tasted. I have often wondered whether this is true – but it is certainly a principle that I have often relied on in making important life choices.

He also said that the '92-94 generation was a "vintage year" which made us proud and yet put some pressure on us to go out into the world and continue to make him proud. He was a wonderful principal, who positively impacted lives with a single speech or a brief exchange.

My sincere condolences to the family.

(51)

End of the year show, 1996. I honestly don't remember much of it, except that we were planning it in Palazzine Dayroom. Someone said "And who's going to do Mr Sutcliffe?"

Total silence.

My English was close to non existent. I was quite shy and, pretty much as everyone else, I was absolutely intimidated by DBS. I still don't know what possessed me to raise my hand, but I volunteered nonetheless.

So the day came, I wore one of my friend's suits, put a ton of baby powder on my hair and went onto the stage. I just remember doing that little bouncy thing he used to do at assemblies, that rocking back and forth motion with his squeaky shoes, holding a blue paper in my hands. What I said (or how I said it), I cannot recall.

As I did my impression, I do remember his steely eyes, folded arms and frozen expression. Towards the end of it, I could see a half smile creeping across his face. But I could be wrong ...

The show ended, and the party ensued. To my surprise, Mr Sutcliffe came to me and invited me to dance with him. Needless to say, that's all the validation 17 year old me needed. This picture is a sweet reminder of that moment, and of all the validation he gave us as students, as human beings.

One of the things I treasure the most from him was the freedom he gave us – freedom to speak up and to make our own choices.

And in that sense, Mr Sutcliffe's leadership style truly shaped the way I undertook my adult life.

(52)

I have a very clear memory of DBS, it was the fall of 1992 I believe, me and my room mates (Villa Mac) decided it would be a good idea to use the TV Room for the evening and leave behind some stuff (cans etc) rather than cleaning up like good boys would/should do. Someone else will clean up, I guess that was the thought process for 17 years old ...

Anyhow the following day the 4 of us were summoned to DBS' office, and I think he only asked a very simple question „Do you think that was the right thing to do, leaving your crap around?" (I am sure he did not use a word like crap), to which I immediately replied „No sir, sorry, it will never happen again!" the whole encounter lasted literally less than 5 minutes but I know I felt like going into a fire-breathing dragon's lair, and making it out alive ... a lesson you do not forget and 27 years later I still have not.

He is sorely missed.

(53)

I vividly remembered my first encounter with him. My Norwegian co-year and I were driven down by her uncle and his friend who had been a student at AC when Sutcliffe was there.

After a long dinner down by the harbour we ended up in the courtyard of Foresteria, and he came out to tell us to keep quiet. When he saw his old student he said «I should have known it was you!».

I was mortified that the first impression my headmaster had of me was slightly drunk, loud and associated with someone who had obviously been a pain in his butt .

(54)

In College Mr Sutcliffe and me didn't have the easiest relationship, so to say. Immature, somehow extreme and quite sensitive I was, coming from a difficult background. It took quite a journey.

He never dropped me out of his heart though.

In a strict way he gave me most valuable advice: „Write, communicate, go on scene, work on your self-discipline.“

Duino stays unshakebly linked to him. And to Kurt Hahn, his mentor.

The older I got the more I was fascinated by his tremendous energy and his capacity to vision.

Through the book-project „Pioneers – how to transmit from one generation to the other?“ Jale and me could make a two days interview with him. From there on a warmly pen-friendship developed.

David Sutcliffe, Adriaan and many other committed persons created a school in Mostar that is different to the globally flourishing service schools for the rich. Born hiddenly – almost like little Jesus – maybe in order to grow up safe? – it is breathing the initial UWC energy, humbly wanting to heal.

A lighthouse has gone; now it is up to us.

(55)

Quando un educatore ottiene cosi tanti riconoscimenti da cosi tanti studenti e studentesse c'è poco da aggiungere: vuol dire che è stato qualcuno che ha svolto benissimo il suo compito e , soprattutto, una persona per bene. E non vi è dubbio che Davd Sutcliffe è stato entrambe le cose.

Ripensando, dopo cosi tanto tempo, a quel biennio 1982-1984 confesso che il ricordo che ho di lui è alquanto sfocato: altri e altre sono state le persone che hanno avuto in qualche modo un'influenza sulla mia vita. Detto con un'espressione che non uso spesso "non ci siamo mai presi".

Credo sia dovuto a un conflitto, anche duro, che avemmo su un episodio che riguardava un altro studente. Gli dissi francamente quello che pensavo sul suo comportamento, mi disse in modo altrettanto franco che stavo sbagliando e che non avrebbe più accettato critiche simili. Mi chiese soltanto il massimo riserbo e quando vide che lo rispettavo sei mesi dopo, un periodo in cui non ci eravamo rivolti parola, mi venne a stringere la mano, senza dire nulla, soltanto che avrei dovuto da grande fumare la pipa! sei un tipo da pipa!

Molti anni dopo ci incontrammo in una riunione commemorativa di quell'esperienza: fu gentile, mi chiese quanti libri avevo letto nel frattempo e di nuovo, all' improvviso, in una pausa della riunione, mi prese da parte e mi chiese perché a mio giudizio " a suo tempo non ci capimmo".

Gli spiegai che la mia insofferenza di allora riguardava più il contesto che la sua persona, la mia sensazione che la storia, quella importante, passasse lontano da Duino. Sorrise senza capirmi. "Ma in realtà mi sbagliavo, eravamo seduti sull'arsenale di Gladio e non lo sapevamo". "Gladio?" Gli spiegai cos'era, la strategia della tensione, che forse dall'arsenale di Aurisina era uscito il tritolo di Piazza Fontana, i dubbi di Calabresi, la sua uccisione. "Eravamo seduti sulla storia, ma ero troppo ingenuo per capirlo".

Non so quanto veramente comprese e se ne parlo' con Belci come gli dissi di fare. Ma mi sembro' sollevato, sereno malgrado le tragedie personali. Sereno come chi era convinto, in fondo, di avere fatto bene quello che bisognava fare. E leggere i commenti pubblicati in questo gruppo gli avrebbe fatto enormemente piacere.

Un uomo verticale, credo si dica in spagnolo!

(56)

My interactions with Mr Sutcliffe in the College were mostly about the daily greetings and his occasional checks on my academic progress. I was not a "trouble" student (I managed to save trouble for later in my grown up life) and my Polish school had instilled in me a healthy respect for and fear of authority. I found the notion of socialising with the headmaster difficult to accept and put into practice.

In the usual twist of fate, I got to know Mr Sutcliffe better after the College when I met him at a number of IB events, including one organised by me in Warsaw. At the time he was exploring ways to make IB more accessible to schools in Central and Eastern Europe. He was concerned with the costs of the programme for schools in that part of the world and wondered about a possibility of creating a "cheaper" version of IB, without compromising its quality and unique characteristics. He believed IB could benefit from a wider participation of Eastern European students but also thought that it could provide a breath of fresh air for the fossilised educational systems of the former socialist countries.

I last met Mr Sutcliffe in Duino in the spring of 2001. I walked into his office with a proposal to organise an international summer course in the College and found out to my great disappointment that he was leaving his post and Duino.

Mr Sutcliffe listened to me and said that he liked the idea and would recommend the project to the new headmaster.

When I got in touch with the College later that year, all had been arranged (following personal recommendation by Mr Sutcliffe).

I was touched because I am sure he had a lot on his mind and plate during the last months of being the headmaster and yet, he kept his promise to me and made it all happen. I ended up in Duino for a number of summers afterwards and never forgot that it was his vision and sense of responsibility that enabled it.

(57)

After graduating from UWC I returned to my native Hungary for university studies. I felt lucky to be so close to Duino still and also dropped back for a long weekend in late autumn – it was the year when the (in)famous date of 7th November was the day of the Eastern European Evening. Of course there had to be grappa brought (well, smuggled in) from Slovenia. During the show I tried to make myself useful lingering around the stage, assisting performers when my first year con-national István surprised (literary) everyone by shoving down quite an amount of a suspicious looking transparent liquid on stage during his scene from a glass bottle.

As he staggered down he let go of it – it landed in my hands (better than on the floor), releasing an unmistakable smell. At that very moment, out of nowhere, DBS stepped right next to me, looking straight into my eyes and scaring the hell out of me.

"Mineral water, of course, isn't it?!", he said in very cool and matter-of-fact way, as if lending me the excuse to save me from trouble.

"Yes! ... mineral water", I said and backed away as quickly as I could.

In 2010-2011 I was given the wonderful opportunity to apply and get shortlisted for a teaching job at the college. I was told there were only the two of us left to select from and invited for a 'trial month' of a shadow teaching experience. I felt my dream was coming true, regardless of the outcome (I got turned down.) Without getting into much detail about the 4 weeks in spring 2011 let me just share that throughout my time there I utterly missed the general feeling of 'family' I had been so nostalgic for.

I tried to decipher its roots in many aspects of college life, through many conversations with students, old and new staff members and I concluded that it had been triggered and kept up by the dedicated, visionary, tireless work of – David B. Sutcliffe. Having experienced Duino as a student with his leadership and as a prospective teacher without him I dare say that he was the motor of that wonderful academic, educational and personal, life-changing experience that so many of us cherish about Duino.

I have taught (and hopefully will teach) in a few schools but never ever have I come across another headmaster of his quality.

(58)

Squeaky shoes, fast walker, bounding onto the morning assembly stage.

And I never realised how young he was while I was a student at Atlantic College 71-73.

(59)

What a fit of nostalgia for those early years! One sentence on David Sutcliffe's write-up kept ringing in my ears, with echoes in my heart. David wrote: "... *forge real daily links with our neighbours*".

That was a purpose he had himself forged in his heart and will. Duinese friends told us that David had come to Duino when the college was not yet there, and he rambled around until he did get to talk to villagers and find a way to identify the natural leaders. He contacted them already to prepare the grounds for forging those links.

Recently, whenever he came to Duino, on every occasion he talked to the locals and most times we did not know that David had been around; it was the Duinese friends who told us that. I want to think that those links he left well forged remain so today and our students keep learning from the few remaining elderly folks who endured the Second World War, when all able-bodied in the village were taken to forced labour and many others, particularly women, taken to extermination camps.

Of the five ladies in the village that had survived Auschwitz and Dachau when the college was open in Duino there is only one alive today and she remains attached to our household as Ximena's social service. She gave us an olive tree to keep in our garden and she told us "look at the tree from time to time and spare a thought for Adele, when I shall no longer be around."

The main way of forging those links was the social service our students offered to old folks in the village. Being with the elderly in Duino was not only a service our students rendered but also a treasure they received from gentle elders resembling their grandparents and acting like them. Besides the affection received, which they baldly needed when far from home, they also learned bits of history and the conversation with them reinforced the learning of the local language. It would be unimaginable that a human being would spend two years in a place and would not learn the local language.

I thank David for having forged those links as we still benefit from them when we visit the village which, in many ways, is also our village.

(60)

The other day when I heard the sad news of DBS' passing, I was poking around the internet to look for news about him and came across this old article about the Atlantic College lifeboats that have such a long and distinguished history, and that DBS helped develop.

I first met David at the Atlantic College, where I spent two summers as the kid brother to Marcello Topa, AC 77-79. I was of course completely intimidated by him, and by the epic stories surrounding him (yes, he did cross the Atlantic solo in a sailboat, and even the most hardened lifeboat drivers in the rough waters outside St. Donat's Castle – who looked larger than life to my tiny 15-year-old self – spoke in hushed tones when they talked about DBS).

Little did I know that he would then be MY headmaster, in Duino (83-85). There too, even though he had considerably mellowed since his days at the Atlantic College, he still had those steely eyes and intense focus (and I was still completely intimidated!).

David had a great influence on all of us, and set a worthy example to follow. I will always remember, in more recent years, his focus on broadening the reach of the UWCs to include refugees: those who have experienced first hand the horrors of war and who literally embody the value of the UWC ideals.

(61)

Sometime in 1976 another student, Leonardo Bracho and I were invited to his house for dinner in AC to welcome a Venezuelan "ambassador" who came to learn about UWC to later start the college in Venezuela. I walked in with shredded jeans, as they were too long for me, and I can't forget his disapproval look. Still he kept that British attitude and dinner went on. Later we became quite close.

(62)

Few people had greater impact on my life than Mr Sutcliffe, who was the founder and headmaster of the high-school I attended in Italy.

He and his radically progressive ideals have shaped me into a far better person than I would have been otherwise, or without the school he created. He taught us to rely on ourselves and each other, and to respect and cherish our differences.

He was a dominant, sometimes intimidating presence in the school. He commanded respect (combined with varying levels of fear) in us students, but treated us as his own family really. He was strict and caring – just as a headmaster should be.

I am sad that he left us forever.

Good bye, Mr Sutcliffe!

(63)

"I was beginning to think that perhaps Sri Lankans were phantom people!' quipped David, when I met him upon my arrival in Duino. In his time as founding head-master of UWC Adriatic, he had some 50+ countries represented in Duino in the early years itself – still, he worked tirelessly, to add a little island nation to the portfolio. It took him repeated scholarship offers over eight full years, before the first Sri Lankan finally arrived in Duino. At that first meeting, he also thanked me profusely for coming to the college, and even wrote to my parents soon after, to thank them for supporting my uptake of the UWC experience. Ironical – it is I who owe it to him.

Thank you, David. You exemplified leadership through human values, completeness of vision, and determination to execute.

(64)

Mr Sutcliffe, la ricorderemo sempre! con affetto dalle "mule" di Duino.

(65)

DBS definitely changed our lives. Maybe it was UWC and not him but that's a pointless question since UWC=DBS in my mind.

Thinking about my 16yo self in Duino, I remember a shy and low self-esteemed girl, coming from a 600 people village, surrounded by beautiful, intelligent, and interesting people.

During my first year I thought the headmaster didn't even know my name ... how wrong I was!!! He knew everything about everybody ...

One of my fondest memories is him threatening me while, at the same time, showing me he really was caring. I was up to no good with my project week and I met him along the road to Motel Agip.

He stopped me and, with a stern and sweet look at the same time, simply said:"Is your mother aware of what you are planning?"

I was dumbstruck by the fact that he knew who I was, my plans, and my family situation. I had never dared to speak to him before.

I still use the telling my mother threat as a measure of the appropriateness of my behaviours and sometimes I used the same threat with my sons' friends, each time thinking about him.

I now realize how free and nurtured at the same time he let us be. He made me feel the world a cosy place.

Thank you, Mr Sutcliffe.

(66)

Reading the comments about David's death, I was surprised at how many people wrote the same thing and felt that David had changed their lives. He brought new experiences into my life and changed my worldview too.

I had horrible war experiences and lived with my family as a refugee (1993-1997) in Germany for four years. I returned to a war devastated Mostar in the summer of 1997.

I met David and George Walker (he was the Director General of the International Baccalaureate at the time) in Mostar, 2004

This was when I was the Chair of the School Board of Mostar Gymnasium (which was the first and only school that had students from two nationalities attending it and sharing the same space since the war from 1992-1995.) As a former Gymnasium student myself, I had a strong desire to contribute to getting life in Bosnia and Herzegovina and specifically Mostar, back to normal. The story of UWC was absolutely unknown to me.

David "captured" me with his story about what the UWC is and what he was trying to accomplish in Mostar; and now I am already in my third term as the Chair of UWC Mostar College Board.

People are writing about David's talents, but I am a witness to the immense persuasion power he had.

With his charisma, enthusiasm and positive energy, he managed to convince me (a lawyer who was volunteering in education) and had weak English skills, to accept the role of Chair of a College board where English was the official language with members who are fluent English speakers.

One of my favorite memories of David was the organizing of his farewell from the position of the Chair of the Foundation that founded UWC Mostar.

On that occasion, I organised a dinner at my house and invited some of the board members. The invitation stated that it was David's "divorce party" (my english).

David joked that he could not remember the wedding at all ...

(67)

One more memory ... at AC, randomly a student had to do a morning reading at Brandestoke hall during the morning assembly ... so one day it was my turn ... I chose to read Jethro Tull's Aqualung backside of the LP cover ... "in the beginning man created God and gave Him a multitude of names" ... another "look" from David Sutcliffe but fine.

(68)

That was in Europa Hotel, marina di Aurisina, 1982, where we started the first days of UWC Adriatic. DBS realised how homesick I was, he spent sometime listening to me with great empathy.

Later, he invited a group of students to his house nearby with personalised invitation for each. He included in the invitation the statement

"Wisam Shamroukh knows how to find the way to our house".

There, I discovered he made up the whole event to help me recover and just feel like home with the Sutcliffes and the rest of my colleagues.

(69)

I never met him. But I grew up with stories about an amazing figure, who was above all a "teacher" in the whole sense what this word might mean. I wish I had met him, although I am happy I learnt and I am still learning through all of you. I hope that his example will be followed by our UWC community, by becoming less politically correct (when necessary) and more of this human being who will stand by our current and future generations in order to form self conscious, determined, powerful and above all good people for the community they will come out to, after our beloved bubble.

My sincere condolences and love to his family and our members of the UWC family who were lucky to live with and learn from him.

(70)

It was such a privilege to have known David Sutcliffe and work under his leadership. I remember when I first met him in Sarajevo exactly 8 years ago, we would go to meetings together and he would generally speak little. He would take short notes in his small black notebook. But when we would leave the meeting he would always amaze me with his remarkable perceptions and instincts. They were always correct, even if that became evident after some time.

I am so thankful for his leadership and never ending passion for the movement, especially UWC Mostar. I last saw him in London two years ago, we had tea. He still had his small black notebook and asked many questions about Mostar.

(71)

Back in 1994 DBS was going on a Balkans tour and participated to final colloquia with potential students. So here is this serious well dressed man asking some questions (later I understood how important were those "casual" ones) . At one point he asks me "so what can you tell me about your hometown"?

Since I come from the town where the best beer in ex Yugoslavia was made, understandably other Montenegrin committee members had started to show some signs of nervosism. I desperately tried to find something else but at the end, trying to be as cool as I could (I was terrified) I said:

"Well Sir, with all due respect we make excellent beer."

Total silence.

After few seconds without absolutely changing the ice cold face he says:

"Well thank you, young man, it is very hot and I will try it as soon as I can!"

(72)

One of my favorite memories is sitting in the front passenger seat of an AC college van as DBS drove us to Fort Bovisand.

I was in charge of the tape recorder and keeping his favorite driving music (at least on that trip) "streaming." It was Beethoven's 9th Symphony.

I have listened to it more than 100 times since, hearing something new each time, and always having a little flashback to that driving & diving trip.

Condolences to the family and all who grieve.

(73)

Once I was walking down Foresteria descendant eating an orange. I dropped a piece of orange peel. And I didn't pick it up. Like a hawk he arrived close to me and taking the fallen peel he said in a icy tone:

I'll pick it up for you.'

At that time I was really shy and slim.

I used not to eat too much and I was probably very focused on the orange. I felt deeply humiliated but not angry because he was right.

He used to be equally strict in both big and minor stuff, but right.

That was I think one of his major strength.

It's more than 30 years and I still think about him anytime I drop something. And I pick it up right away ... anytime.

(74)

It seems significant that the strongest Duino memories I have of him were connected to sharing activities with students, although I also saw much to admire from my DOS office. David heading down to the porto to the boats, I to the cliffs for some climbing, both totally content that this was as important as any academic pursuit.

So I will share a memory of how he appeared when away from Duino, at a large conference we both attended (I think it was IB in Kopenhagen).

David was on the stage, part of a panel discussion. While all the other worthies expressed satisfaction and pride in what the IB had achieved, David calmly and to great effect and some annoyance outlined why he considered the IB to have failed in an important way. He spoke about students in Soweto, about how inaccessible this expensive programme was to them and needy young people all over, and challenged the IB and other boards of international school organisations to come up with creative and affordable solutions. He was not diplomatic but blisteringly honest.

Well, the IB never could live up to this challenge, never developed alternatives for Soweto.

It is so encouraging that the UWCs still pursue their mission to which David has given so much.

(75)

It is more than likely that whoever might have been in long term contact with David Sutcliffe might have had to endure the arduous task of deciphering his cryptic notes scribbled with his hand.

As a historian my training included the art of paleography and I have no great difficulty in reading old Spanish colonial manuscripts.

But on occasions I declared myself defeated with David's notes and had to seek desperate help from Elizabeth so as to make sure that David was or wasn't firing me. Elizabeth always smiled at these requests and commented:

"There are occasions when David himself cannot read his own handwriting and asks for my help."

(76)

I was 16 when I was selected for UWCAD, Mr Sutcliffe was in the commission in Trieste.

I was a scared and ordinary Italian girl, spoke little English and had no special experiences ...

... probably he saw something in me that no one, nor myself had knowledge at that time ...

... I will be forever grateful to him for that. He was able to see us all not as immature teenagers, but as the future adults we were soon going to be. He trusted us and let us express ourselves ...

Thanks DBS, you'll always be remembered!

(77)

There are not so many people in this world who are able to put visions into reality with incredible stamina, being truly a force of life. David was certainly one of a few.

Will always be grateful for David being as stubborn as me, giving me endless support in keeping UWC Mostar going on, against all odds.

(78)

A sad day ... Strange how years had to pass before I realised how much he cared, and how deeply (and successfully) he worked to instill in us core values that we hold dear to our hearts. Thank you, DBS ...

My most sincere condolences to Elisabeth and the family ...

(79)

Caro rettore, I will remember you as a good father of many children, who is there for each one at the right moment, to look me at the eye, respectfully, and tell me just a few, but the words I need.

After many years when I was filling in a survey about leaders in my life, I realised I could hardly recall more then fingers on one hand. And you were one of them. A visionary, persistent, good listener, a good diplomat.

We were difficult to you sometimes, teenagers who were given the freedom to think, speak, act – and we turned sometimes against the one who had the most merits for that won freedom. But you would just quickly rub your face with your palms, go for a walk on Rilke and restore the faith that you are doing the right thing with us.

Thank you so much for being this big person in my life, in our lives.

(80)

Mr Sutcliffe sapeva l'italiano, e lo parlava pure bene, con limitato accento. Però proprio non gli doveva piacere: a Duino si rivolgeva a noi italiani irrimediabilmente in inglese. E io non ci ho capito niente per tutto il primo anno ...

Nonostante questo, non ho mai potuto fare a meno di stimarlo e rispettarlo anche solo per il coraggio di essersi messo alla guida di un collegio "diffuso" come Duino, popolato per lo più da incontrollabili italiani e latino-americani (non propriamente il massimo di disciplina britannica) in preda ai loro ormoni adolescenziali. Ce la faceva benissimo, magari alle volte strigliandoci con uno storico "I am humilated" che ci fece sentire tutti in colpa o riprendendoci uno a uno ("Giorgio, what about coming to your marine activities sometimes?").

Scusate l'uso della lingua di Dante, ma proprio in inglese non riesco a sentire e oggi sono davvero triste.

(81)

I never met Mr Sutcliffe in person but I am forever grateful for the way he changed my life and that of my family. I grew up in the midst of the conflict in Iraq and we barley had any means of survival. It was through his support to UWC Mostar that I was able to escape my circumstances. He sponsored my study for the two years and completely changed my life. I am dedicated to carry his legacy and work on making my country a better place. In doing so, I will always remember him every step of the way.

Rest In Peace.

(82)

And now?

One of his last email messages I received from David, he attached a publication containing his reflections at a moment in his life when he was still active and using his full potential as a human being, in order to bring to fruition the product of his concept of formative educations for our days.

Those were reflections that had to be articulated with force and urgency, not only because of dark forebodings that might have assailed his subconscious, but rather because he was a man of his days – our days – with a clear conscience of the new mission and challenges facing any project of formative education, firmly based on history and its projections for our days and for the future.

It was the publication of papers issued by former members of staff of the International School of Geneva and of Atlantic College under the title "*The International School of Geneva and the United World Colleges in the early years of the International Baccalaureate*". The publication contains four essays, two of them written by David and all four were related to the commemoration of the 50th Anniversary of the International Baccalaureate. It was published in August, 2018. The title above – "And Now? – is one that David himself used for his main piece. No need for further explanation because David's own words convincingly convey the main challenge for formative education in our days, which can be clearly grasped by reading the following excerpt:

....

"A fifty-year anniversary is not a time for regrets, but it is surely a moment at which to relate past achievement to future challenge. In the clear if jargon-tainted words of one writer, we face 'a new global context and the requirement for shared norms for the new reality'. So perhaps this is the moment when the IB, the UWC and international education generally, busy though they legitimately are in meeting the needs of the thousands of mobile families worldwide, should be seeking to identify their future role if they are to remain pacemakers in confronting 'the new reality' ...

I begin by wondering, first, why we have not made an impact on immigrant and multi-cultural inner-city schools. Here are the hard realities of inter-racial and inter- cultural learning, all too often against a background of financial and social deprivation. The number of IB inner-city state schools in the United States is impressive. Is their experience being brought to bear in fellow IB schools elsewhere? Surely the lessons must be rich and revealing. The figures suggest that Europe has much catching up to do, but the explanation is straightforward: the cost. State schools in European cities with large racially mixed and immigrant communities cannot afford the IB.

I wonder, second, how we confront the challenges of the developing world, how we stand compared with, for example, Seema Aziz of Paki-

stan who, against all local tradition and to her family's dismay, opened her first clothes shop at the age of 34 in Lahore's ancient cloth market, now runs an empire of 450 stores and, more importantly for us, today operates 256 schools 'to give a sound education to boys and girls who would otherwise be illiterate ... her CARE schools are now starting to change Pakistan itself, helping this beautiful but damaged country to make use of the abundant talents of its population'. Her aim is expansion until they are teaching one million children."

....

David's second paper follows a similar tenor and he included this poem by the English-American poet Wystan Hugh Auden written in the 1930th: (I have added its title)

....

REFUGEE BLUES

"Once we had a country and we thought it fair,
Look in the atlas and you'll find it there:
We cannot go there now, my dear, we cannot go there now.
The consul banged the table and said,
"If you've got no passport, you're officially dead":
But we are still alive, my dear, but we are still alive.
Went to a committee; they offered me a chair;
Asked me politely to return next year:
"If we let them in, they will steal our daily bread":
But where shall we go to-day, my dear, but where shall we go today?
Came to a public meeting; the speaker got up and said;
He was talking of you and me, my dear,
he was talking of you and me."

....

Not much to add.

(83)

I remember when Mr Sutcliffe and his colleague came to Mostar in the Office of the High Representative in 2002/2003 ... not sure. He wanted to talk to someone from our office, Head of Political Unit, about the UWC movement and possibility to establish the College in Mostar.

As my supervisor was out of the office, for I was in that time Political Officer in the OHR, and not being aware of who Mr Sutcliffe was, I offered a drink and readiness to hear what his visit was about ... aiming to transfer the message to my boss, as we usually do it when important guests visit OHR.

As I was a child of former Yugoslavia, I remember that I never heard about UWC, a movement which Mr Sutcliffe started to explain. I was delighted with the idea and asked many questions and he joyfully answered.

He than said that there is an idea to establish the UWC College in Mostar, but he wanted to hear about the political situation in Mostar, the political climate in general, key figures in the institutions, the extent of support for the movement from the International Community etc.

While he was presenting the initiative, I realised that I must invest all my efforts and undertake something. It was a foggy, unclear vision in my head when he spoke about "that UWC" but I said to myself "I use all my connections within the office, particularly in domestic institutions in that time, to push for this idea, for these people, this man can make something good and bring something great to Mostar" ... not knowing what the idea actually would look like in Mostar. I only sensed that UWC, in a way he described it, would be great for BiH, for Mostar, for students, our children, newer generations.

Mr Sutcliffe was so convincing in his presentation about a new education and the diversity of culture, various chances, joint life of different ethnicities, that I told him I will try to speak with my supervisors. And that is how this all started ...

Mr Sutcliffe invited me later to join the National Committee of UWC Mostar.

Had I not met Mr Sutcliffe and his friend at that time, at that specific moment, I would have missed a chance to be part of this wonderful journey of the UWC movement. I never had the opportunity to thank him for everything he had done for initiative, action and establishment of UWC Mostar. I am very, very proud to have known him, I will always remember our first accidental talk about UWC. Simply said, it was meant to be!

Rest in peace!

(84)

At this moment, as I try to keep my sorrow over David's death at bay, I remember our first contacts and meetings. It was seventeen years ago that among the heap of official mail at the Department for International Cooperation in Education, Science and Culture that I headed at the Bosnian Ministry of Foreign Affairs, I found an unusual letter. It had not been sent by an institution, as most other letters to the Ministry. It was a personal letter, from an individual, signed "David B. Sutcliffe". The letter had evidently gone from one department to another at the Ministry before it reached mine. In it, the undersigned gentleman talked about founding a United World College in BiH, said he was coming to visit Sarajevo and asked to meet with people who could be of assistance.

That was how we met started working together on improving secondary and pre-university education in BiH for the next fifteen years, first as part of the Executive Board of the UWC-IBO Initiative in BiH, and then within the Governing Board of the Education in Action Foundation. Throughout that time, David Sutcliffe was a driving force, the source of a wealth of experience, someone you went to for advice, someone who was always prepared to discuss problems and never gave up on finding solutions.

David dedicated his life to the education of young people at United World Colleges, an education that brings together young people from all over the world in order to do away with divisions and inequalities, put an end to wars and enable lasting peace in the world, and for that we shall remain forever grateful to him.

Prof L. T.

Foundation „Education in Action" – Founder and Executive Director

(85)

I must confess I knew very little about Mostar College.

It was David who impressed on me how important the project was for him and in his emails emphasised so forcefully his commitment to see it fully settled as part and parcel of Mostar itself, not as a foreign enclave detached from the local history, culture and the people there, still permeated by the echoes of a war.

There must be there a symbol for reconciliation and Mostar College could well be a force for unity, progress and profound reconciliation for a brutally fragmented society, not in the territory but in the mentality. I have quoted part of his emails, and I have more of them. They made a strong impression on my conscientiousness because I had never realised the potential a college can have in that environment.

(86)

"A turquoise A4 paper that David presented in his office in Italy in late 2000 was titled 'United World College of Eastern Europe in Mostar – First thoughts'. I still have the document.

I was visiting my old school, Adriatic college, five years since graduating to talk to students about my research work in Bosnia and Herzegovina (David always welcomed his students back).

During the lunch in the beautiful Porto (David was a great host) I challenged David about his speech in a Prague UWC meeting some weeks earlier where he had mentioned UWC should go "where it is needed and cannot be afforded" and mentioned the need to develop UWC role in the new and profoundly challenging context of Bosnia and Herzegovina.

I asked David what he had in mind as he never suggested anything without having already a plan. He admitted no plan as yet but we started discussing. David invited me to his office two hours later. Meanwhile he had written the turquoise memo signed "D.B.S. 12th November 2000".

David described our meeting in Duino later: "From this reciprocal provocation emerged six years later the United World College in Mostar."

This collection of memories – the Prague event, my visit soon after to Duino, the lunch and the "provoked" turquoise paper – are among the dearest memories I have. While I had been working with David – or Mr Sutcliffe as we always referred to him with respect – as a student in Duino 1993-95, this chain of events five years later led him to become my mentor, a colleague and a very special friend.

Over the last 18 years – most intensively 2001-2006 – we worked together a lot and often on daily basis in Helsinki-London-Sussex-Sauris-Sarajevo also spending quite some time together in Bosnia and Herzegovina. David brought his important friend Antonin B. Besse to the team from the start and we were often referred to as "three musketeers" (I also had a chance to follow two passionate and intelligent men debating – to the extent of even having a period of no-contact at some point). In 2016 I followed David as the chair of the board of Education in Action, the foundation in charge of UWC in Mostar.

As a first hand witness I want to stress: without David's passion, commitment, leadership, personal charisma and simply hard work UWC Mostar would never have been conceptualised as a project in 2001, opened in 2006 and kept alive through the financial crisis.

We both felt we did something very special together and we also knew that our work for five years on personal volunteer basis was critical as was David's idea to seek money for me to move to Bosnia with my family in 2005 for 1,5 years to give our project a serious try.

As critical was the continues persistence of David through the most difficult years with the key people on the ground – Jasminka Bratic, Valentina Mindoljevic, Lamija Tanovic, Mirna Jancic, Velema Roksa – just to mention a few. The staff members were incredible too.

Memories are many. Some serious, some funny, many very important, many very personal. I will try to collect them in due course. Two things I want to say here. Fist, David always remembered to underline the contribution of my husband and family just as he would always mention his wife's Elisabeth's role in everything. They did things together. Second, David respected people for what they were.

He met my non-English speaking countryside Father, Grandmother and poor Sarajevan landlady in her small flat and left strong impression on all of them. People were people to him. David wrote to me in August 2019 "please do not worry too much about me". During these months I have said to my parents and husband that my emotional reaction tells it all. I loved David deeply. The same way I now miss him. I notice, however, that the enormous sadness transforms gradually into immeasurable gratitude for having been able to get to know him and to work with him.

I believe his influence will guide the actions and life choices of mine and incredibly many people also during the years to come.

*"Education must enable young people to effect
what they have recognised to be right,
despite hardships, despite dangers, despite inner skepticism,
despite boredom, and despite mockery from the world"*

(Kurt Hahn)

List of tributors:

(AC = Atlantic College, UWCAD = United College of the Adriatic)

1) Manuel Fernandez Canque, teacher, founder of the social services at UWCAD (83-03)
2) Manuel Fernandez Canque
3) Elaine Teo (UWCAD 94-96)
4) Alex Neuber (UWCAD 83-85)
5) Alexander Grubic Wirtz (UWCAD 94-96)
6) Patrik Brundin (AC 78-80)
7) Mette Høie (UWCAD 86-88)
8) Jan Carl Adelswärd (UWCAD 86-88)
9) Julie Koch (UWCAD 88-90)
10) Frederico Rosei (UWCAD 88-90)
11) Bora Toska (Red Cross Nordic United World College 01-03)
12) Manuel Fernandez Canque
13) Manuel Fernandez Canque
14) Amit Mohindra Son of Captain Raj Mohindra founding chief executive of Mahindra UWC in India
15) Marcel Mikolášik (UWCAD 96-98)
16) Paul Birighitti. (UWCAD 84-86)
17) Yew Chin Tan Eugene (UWCAD 99-01)
18) Lu Xina Torres (UWCAD 99-01)
19) Tanya Behrisch (UWCAD 86-88)
20) Laura Amescua (UWCAD 85-87)
21) Sergio Vasques (UWCAD 87-89)
22) Lamija Tanovic
23) Michał Gwardyś
24) Adriaan van Otterloo (UWCAD 87-89)
25) Anders Dahlbeck (UWCAD 97-99)
26) Marvic Francalanza (UWCAD 94-96)
27) Gerhard Schneider (AC 77-79)
28) Amanda Fong (UWCAD 95-97)

29) Assia Brandrup (AC 72-74)
30) Demet Devrim Derbil (UWCAD 86-88)
31) Giulio Federico (UWCAD 90-92)
32) Diana Bebek Ivankovic (UWCAD 84-86)
33) Ximena Pineda Teacher and co-founder of the social services at UWCAD (83-02)
34) Tvrtko Cernos (UWCAD 88-90)
35) Roberta Secchi (UWCAD 86-88)
36) Mauro Casiraghi (UWCAD 88-90)
37) Luiz Antonio Magalhaes (UWCAD 87-89)
38) Maria Gallotti (UWCAD 90-92)
39) Silva Tomanic Kis (AC 79-81)
40) Nicholas Isaacs (Music Instructor at AC 73-77)
41) Alain Mauri (UWCAD 88-90)
42) Darina Dujmic (UWCAD 88-90
43) Adriaan van Otterloo (UWCAD 87-89)
44) Anne Nielsen
45) Robert Tomalin (UWCAD 95-97)
46) Jen Van Ellemeet (AC 74-76)
47) Valérie Henry Lavigne
48) Massimo Lengo (UWCAD 85-87)
49) Sami Jarrar (UWCAD 84-86)
50) Daria Miglietta Ferrari (UWCAD 92-94)
51) Ceci Egan (UWCAD 95-97)
52) Eugenio Filippi (UWCAD 91-93)
53) Ingrid Prytz Ohm (UWCAD 87-89)
54) Marc Glorius (UWCAD 86-88)
55) Leonardo Casalino (UWCAD 82-84)
56) Marcin Zaleski (UWCAD 87-89)
57) Kató Eszter (UWCAD 95-97)
58) Pastor Linda Theophilus (AC 71-73)
59) Manuel Fernandez Canque
60) Giorgio Topa (UWCAD 83-85)
61) Pedro Herrera-Iglesias

62) Attila Kovacs (UWCAD 91-93)
63) Dhakshi Ravishankar
64) Fabiana Coslovich (Secretary at UWCAD)
65) Renata Bolognini (UWCAD 86-88)
66) Jasmins Tanovic-Bratic
67) Pedro Herrera-Iglesias
68) Wisam Shamroukh (UWCAD 82-84)
69) Niovi Zarampouka-Chatzimanou (UWCAD 06-08)
70) Elma Mahmutovic
71) Milorad Samardzic (UWCAD 94-96)
72) Sara Payne (AC 72-74)
73) Marina Macchiaiolo (UWCAD 86-88)
74) Walther Hetzer (Director of studies UWCAD 85-91)
75) Manuel Fernandez Canque
76) Marilli Genova (UWCAD 83-85)
77) Valentina Mindolijevic
78) John Alexandropoulos
79) Branka Uskokovic Zizic (UWCAD 90-92)
80) Giorgio Casanova (UWCAD 84-86)
81) Mohammed M. Obaid Shwani (UWC Mostar 17-19)
82) Manuel Fernandez Canque
83) Amela Bozic
84) Lamija Tanovic
85) Manuel Fernandez Canque
86) Dr. Pilvi Torsti, Chair of Foundation Education in Action, UWCAD 1993-95 & co-founder of UWC Mostar

Think afar: Education needs inspiration

"My suggestion is that we have behind (I include the UWCs in my reflection) the achievement of excellence. We now face the challenge of *relevance"* (David Sutcliffe 2001).

During a college meeting David stood in front of a world map.

"We have Atlantic College," he said, "we have a college in Scandinavia, we have the Adriatic College, we have one in the Far East. We don't have one in the Middle East. A college in the Middle East would be important. It would contribute to the peace process."

How could he attribute such high importance to small boarding schools like the UWCs?

Another sentence from him, I memorised:

"Think about our grandchildren going to the College."

At its beginnings, the college was playing a pioneer role. A school with students coming to Italy to the Adriatic coast from all over the world on full scholarship basis, this made my surroundings prick up their ears – and dream.

UWC teachers were also pioneers. Franziska Raimund developed a unique Language department. Richard van de Lagemaat published for the IB the reference textbook on TOK. John Plommer designed the "World Arts and Cultures Course". Or just remembering Elham Sheiry sitting in the bar surrounded by coffee-drinking and cigarette-smoking students, walking up and down, and him explaining, discussing, "breathing" mathematics. Manuel and Ximena Fernandez, who created a wonderful network of social services, deeply anchoring the school in the bosom of the community.

The entire school going with half the village on a trip to Vienna.

These are only some examples.

This school tried something new and different. It was – said with some pathos – a star on the horizon of international and national education.

And today: How can one keep, revive, and develop this legacy of being a pioneer?

How can it continue to play a pioneer role in "experiential education"?

"Without the instinct of adventure, any civilization however enlightened; any state, however well-ordered, will wilt and wither" (Kurt Hahn)

(A) Sustainability

The topic of this book is transmission between generations. How can a sustainable approach express itself on this behalf? To put some humor with it: Human body is sustainable. As corpse it is put into soil and then transformed to organic matter which generates new life. How is the legacy of one generation best transmitted to the other?

First thing to realize is that the purpose of UWC as an educational organization is trans-generational. UWC definitely will need several generations to fulfill its „mission" which implies that understanding between the generations is necessary in order „to pass the baton".

Understanding implies openness and the readiness to reflect one's prejudices towards each other. The younger generations don't „have to reinvent the wheel" each time, the older generations let go the attitude of "everything was better before".

The legacy is the essence of intention and experience – which is timeless somehow. Navigation to a world of peace and bliss – the mission of UWC – can be difficult. It gets facilitated if you add „Where do I come from?" to the question „Where do I go to?"

While I am writing these lines there is – again – a war going on in Europe and there is the threat of the use of nuclear weapons. (Hopefully this threat will not be there anymore, when the book gets published.) While I am writing these lines climate change is having more and more devastating effects. The destruction caused by it is getting tangible globally.

While I am writing these lines awareness is rising about the global "soil crisis" threatening the entire planet with massive famines and migration movements.

We are facing a dramatic escalation of the worldwide situation. Two exits are left. Either we say no to life and continue like before. This will lead to our extinction.

Or we say yes!, develop our civilizations into sustainable cultures and get more conscious about who and what we are. To live in harmony with yourself, the others and the planet is the central issue of sustainability. It is fairly challenging to reach this cultural level.

There exist appropriate solutions to the major problems of our times ranging from quantum physics and the wholistic framework they provide, an inclusive mindset, collective trauma work, to sustainable technologies, regenerative farming, circular economy, canalization of aggression, mindful practices and many more.

"Think about our grandchildren going to the College".

Sustainability cannot be realised by some individuals only. It is a communal task. It needs coorporation. It needs transgenerational understanding.

Sustainability is no way an ideology that can be indoctrinated:

"It is a sin of the soul to force young people into opinions ... but it is culpable neglect not to impel young people into experiences"

(Kurt Hahn)

(B) Talking about the college in Duino and its future:

– Why not align with other movements heading to the same destination?

There exist great global movements whose core issue is sustainability. They mobilize thousands and millions of volunteers, collaborators and activists. I am referring to the Presencing Institute of Otto Scharmer, Thomas Hübl's institute of inner science and the Isha Foundation of Sadhguru. There are many others. How about cooperating with these movements?

– Why not enlarge the circle of the school?

One could involve the ex-students more, for example by offering summer camps and academies or developing "volunteer work opportunities" or even a proper UWC diploma, as "post-graduate" diploma. One could extent the social service structures, develop a language center for the community and an evening school. Why not project housing plans for the alumni generations that are growing older, for possibility to move to the region after their active professional career? For possibility to contribute experience, know-how, and passion to the school and UWC vision?

The school could broaden its basis in general. It could focus on growing into a cultural center with research, workshops, shows and conferences. It would „radiate" into its surroundings in the tradition of numerous Italian medieval and renaissance towns. This would significantly raise the visibility and the presence of the college. Sure: A broader basis of the school would require a bigger budget. On the other hand: Wouldn't a fully tangible relevance of the college be likely to attract significantly more funding?

– And finally: Why not intentionally enforce the "specific architecture" of the College?

"Architecture spécifique" a term coined by Jean Nouvel, Prizker award winning French architect. "Specific architecture" stands out from the easy-to-copy, shapeless globalised constructions. Architecture gets specific by relating consciously and with intent to its context and environment.

David Sutcliffe created the college as a "specific architecture" before the term even existed. He kept emphasizing the importance of the relationships with the village, the region, Italy, ex-Yugoslavia, "Mitteleuropa". The college needs to nourish, cultivate and deepen its capacity to relate: Going from the village to the three boarders, to Italy, to Europe, to the world and far beyond.

I deliberately associate Italy to four phenomena: Renaissance, Arte Povera, San Francesco di Assisi, and Machiavelli. Our times put the wrestle for power, and career success first: Machiavelli. A sustainable culture instead, working to rebalance humanity with nature, is in need of Renaissance.

„Confidence in effort, modesty in success, grace in defeat, fairness in anger, clear judgement, even in the bitterness of wounded pride, readiness to serve at all times".

These educational maxims were expressed by Kurt Hahn who was David Sutcliffe's mentor and co-creator of the Atlantic college in Wales. These maxims express an ethical ideal which is timeless and – like all ideals – difficult to reach. A lot of obstacles stand in its way.

Yet: "Education doesn't want to remove the obstacles. It just wants to make them surmountable" (Kurt Hahn).

Enlarging the circle of the school, enforcing its specific architecture and aligning it with other movements would significantly develop the shape of the college and its impact. It would put it to the next level and open many new possibilities.

"When I set goals my motto is: Reach out to the stars, so you may be able to reach the moon. If you reach out to the moon, you'll be maybe able to reach the top of Mount Everest"

(Dr. Jane Goodall)

"To be alone means turning a fact – each one of us is alone – into a task for life and for thinking. Only then one realizes how difficult it is to distinguish if it is oneself or society that is thinking and feeling"

(R. Safranski – Being alone)

"Live as if you were to die tomorrow
Learn as if you were to live forever"
(Mahatma Gandhi)

Special thanks to:

Doc Martin Haeusler for his tremendous help getting this book
published,
Jale Maria Gönenc for various support and artistic advice,
my father Ulrich Glorius without whom I wouldn't exist,
Manuel Fernandez for the idea to this book,
Julia Plessing for translating
Nike Kunene for proof reading

And to you with whom I experienced these times
Jan, Julia, Susana, Janus, Katja, Soraya, Giorgio M., Iva,
Lucia, Niki, Karin, Tony, Jochen, Michi and also Eline,
Yazan, Luiz, Daniel, Björn, Matteo S. and Barbara!

Each name puts a song in my heart